Feedback and Society

Feedback and Society

A Study of the Uses of Mass Channels for Coping

Benjamin D. Singer
University of Western Ontario and
Dartmouth College

Lexington Books
D.C. Heath and Company
Lexington, Massachusetts
Toronto   London

WITHDRAWN
ITHACA COLLEGE LIBRARY

Library of Congress Cataloging in Publication Data

Singer, Benjamin D.   1931–
    Feedback and society.

    1. Communication– Social aspects.   2. Mass media–
Social aspects. I. Title.
HM258.S485   301.16   73–1016
ISBN 0–669–85423–9

Published simultaneously in Canada.

Printed in the United States of America.

International Standard Book Number: 0–669–85423–9

Library of Congress Catalog Card Number: 73–1016

Table of Contents

List of Tables   vii

Acknowledgements   xi

Chapter 1   The Uses of Feedback   1

Chapter 2   Research into Mass Feedback   9

Chapter 3   Toward an Analysis of Mass Feedback Channels: 21
               The Questions and the Methods

Chapter 4   Letters to the Editor   33

Chapter 5   The Urban Newspaper Ombudsman   41

Chapter 6   The Radio Call-In Show   45

Chapter 7   Some Psychological and other Explanations for
               Participation   57

Chapter 8   The Information Center   67

Chapter 9   Summary and Conclusions   85

Chapter 10   Appendixes   93

               About the Author   121

               Index   123

List of Contents

List of Tables

3.1 Age of Respondents and 1966 London Census Age Breakdown by Sex (Percentage)   23

3.2 Marital Status of Respondents and 1966 London Census Marital Status Data (15 Years and Over)   24

3.3 Religion of Respondents Compared with 1961 Census Data   25

3.4 Education Level of Respondents Compared with Census Education Data   26

3.5 Respondents' Total Family Income from All Sources   27

3.6 Sex and Employment Status of Respondents   27

3.7 Occupational Status Scores of Respondents   28

4.1 Have You Ever Written A Letter to the Letters-to-the-Editor Column in a Newspaper?   34

4.2 How Many Letters Have You Written in the Past Two Years? How Many Were Published?   35

4.3 Sex of Respondents. Have You Ever Written a Letter to the Editor?   36

4.4 Age Distribution of Letter Writers Compared with Sample   36

4.5 Educational Distribution of Letter Writers Compared with Sample   36

4.6 Income Distribution of Letter Writers Compared with Sample   37

4.7 Success in Letter Publishing and Age   39

4.8 Topics of Letter Writers   39

4.9 Purpose of Letters   39

5.1 Education Distribution of "Sound Off" Users Compared with Sample   42

5.2 Over What Issue Did You Contact "Sound Off"?   43

6.1 What Do You Like About Open-Line Programs?   45

6.2 What Do You Dislike About Open-Line Programs?   46

6.3 Frequency of Usage of Phone-In Shows   47

6.4 Age Distributions of Callers and Sample   47

6.5 Education Distributions of Callers and Sample   49

6.6 Income of Callers and Sample   49

6.7	Topics of Open Line Callers	49
6.8	Purpose of Calls fo Open Line	50
6.9	Duration of Calls	51
6.10	Call Stimuli	52
6.11	Proximate Stimulus and Type of Call	53
6.12	Host's Responses to Callers	54
6.13	Host's Responses to Different Kinds of Calls	55
7.1	Anomie Score of Respondents and Writing Letters to a Newspaper	59
7.2	Anomie Score of Respondents and Ever Contacted "Sound Off"	59
7.3	Anomie Score of Respondents and Calling the Open Line	61
7.4	Anomie and Usage by Participation Channels Controlled by Occupational Status	61
7.5	Anomie Rating of Users of Various Participatory Channels	63
7.6	Stimulus Factor for Letters to Editor and Call-In Radio Shows	64
8.1	Sex of Information London Respondents Compared with Census Sex Data for 1966	68
8.2	Age of Information London Respondents Compared with Census Age Data for 1966	69
8.3	Education Level of Information London Respondents Compared with Census Education Data for 1966	71
8.4	Inquiries per Thousand Population by Educational Level	71
8.5	Source of Initial Contact	71
8.6	Channel Used	72
8.7	Type of Inquiry	73
8.8	Categories of Inquiry	73
8.9	Disposition of Inquiries	74
8.10	Channels Used by Males and Females	75
8.11	Inquiry Types by Males and Females	75
8.12	Male-Female Differences in Categories of Inquiry	76
8.13	Male-Female Differences in Disposition of Inquiry	77

8.14	Age and Channels Used	77
8.15	Age and Types of Inquiries	77
8.16	Age and Categories of Inquiry	78
8.17	Age and Disposition	80
8.18	Education and Channel Used	81
8.19	Education and Type of Inquiry	81
8.20	Education and Category of Inquiry	82
8.21	Education and Disposition	83

Acknowledgments

This book is the product of the assistance and advice of many people and organizations. For financial assistance, I am indebted to the Canada Council and the *London Free Press,* which made possible the gathering of the basic data; to the federal Department of Communications for its financial assistance that made possible the analysis and completion of reports, and to Information London personnel for their cooperation and aid. Any opinions expressed, positions taken or errors committed are mine alone and none of the sponsors should be held responsible for them.

My student assistants – Lyndsay Green, Ted Seacrest, Dale Johnston, Andrew Hannigan, and John Hannigan – worked conscientiously and made valuable suggestions, as did project secretary Nina Allinson. They have all since gone on to well-deserved greater things for themselves.

For their critical reading, comments, and good suggestions, I thank Bud Knight, general manager of CFPL radio; Chandler Stevens of Rensselaer Polytechnic Institute; and, especially, Richard Gwyn, Director-General of the Socio-Economic Planning Branch, Department of Communications. Alvin Toffler has been a constant fountainhead of ideas on the broader topic of coping toward which this study is, hopefully, a contribution. I have also had an opportunity to gain an audience during colloquia at the Urban Studies Department, Waterloo University, and the Sociology Department of the University of Vermont, which has been very valuable in working out some of my ideas. In addition, the facilities provided by the Sociology Department of Dartmouth College helped provide the environment necessary to complete the manuscript.

I have always threatened to end an article or book with the line: ". . . however, *less* research is needed in this area." Without question, I cannot do that with this topic.

Feedback and Society

1

The Uses of Feedback

Kenneth E. Boulding has said:

The rise of modern technology and the growth in the complexity of the knowledge structure of the society is perhaps the dominant factor in the political process of modern society. (Boulding, 1971: 107)

Other writers have had similar sentiments about knowledge or information. An important theme in Toffler's *Future Shock* involves the role of information and of the information explosion that now engulfs our society (Toffler, 1970). Going beyond the notion of knowledge or information per se, a current very well-accepted perspective for viewing urban societies sees them as patterns of transactions in which information or knowledge *channels* become the critical variable (Meier, 1962). We are inevitably led to appreciate as one of the most central problems of modern society the growing complexity of the lines of communication between individuals and the institutions upon which they have come to depend for the knowledge they need in order to survive in industrial society.

The present book addresses itself to this kind of problem. It is, in fact, a study in the newly developing Sociology of Coping; however, it directs itself more especially to problems found under the rubric "feedback." It is an attempt to work toward articulating a problem which many of us recognize, but about which little of an empirical nature has been done.

During a time of great change, as organizations proliferate and become more complex, linkages between individuals and organizations upon which they depend become vague, less discernible; and there develops a puzzling contradiction, for, as our society becomes more rationalized in a technological-economic-and-social sense, much more that is important to the individual attempting to cope becomes enmeshed in a grey, ambiguous, difficult-to-define panoply of channels and procedures; people become less sure about their rights, their legitimacy in seeking them, their way of communicating their feelings, opinions, and needs to such institutions and, therefore, to their society.

The social system becomes more "rational" while paths to important institutions become more hazy; because of long lines of communication (the increase in required technical procedures is also a way by which lines become elongated), while ever more obstacles are erected which prevent solid contact with them from below, a strange kind of communications imbalance develops: it

1

becomes easier for governmental and corporate entities to reach us when they wish, less expensive in terms of cost and manpower to communicate *to* us, while at the same time it becomes more difficult for us to make contact with them. Technically, in a democratic society we have the *right* to this contact; practically, in a complex society we often don't know how; or the amount of time and energy it requires discourages us. Ultimately, particularly for the less articulate, the ghetto dwellers, the old, and the needy, this communication imbalance becomes the cause of a profound disengagement from belief in the legitimacy of the social institutions that play paramount roles in maintaining our society. This is one of the more salient definitions of that much abused word, alienation.

We cannot find out about things although we are in the midst of an information explosion. We cannot make our voices heard by those whom we need to hear us. Ultimately, the problems of information seeking, the ombudsman-interventionist function in society, and public opinion expression join empirically and become intertwined theoretically. Not only are they intertwined, but their study becomes, in part, a study of the symptoms of a malaise and in part an answer to the problem.

It has been said that Athenian democracy was in great part made possible by social and physical institutions in an open air environment which promoted constant verbal intercourse and the exchange of views between Greeks (Kitto, 1957: 36-37). In a physically closed-in society, which is also as large as ours, that obviously is not possible. As Chandler Stevens put it:

When we think of dialogue and democracy, we might think of Greek Forums and early New England Town meetings ... (yet) ... it is clear that such meetings cannot now be considered to be major components of a significant dialogue system, that is, one which is specifically designed for this age of high mobility and instant news. (Stevens, 1972)

Does the lack of adequate channels for two-way communication mean that democracy and complex society cannot coexist? Writers such as Hannah Arendt, Franz Neuman, and C. Wright Mills suggest that atomization of the individual precedes the development of totalitarianism, and atomization is facilitated by the lack of channels. And those channels make possible the kind of feedback which, if it exists in an otherwise mass society, would presumably serve to preclude the movement away from democracy. The term *feedback* has gained acceptance as a means for describing the capability for communication to higher levels of authority, although originally it was used by Wiener to mean, in a cybernetic sense, the ability to "adjust future conduct by past performance" (Wiener, 1954: 33). If we were to use the term in the exact way Wiener meant it, half of the meaning is determined by the perfect match of action to past state. Perfect feedback ought to be equated with the perfect democracy.

The term has lent itself to further categorization – *direct* feedback and *indirect* feedback:

The principal means of access to direct feedback channels are: elections, political parties, lobbies and other special interest and pressure groups, letters, phone calls, and visits to elected representatives and government offices, public opinion polls, and demonstrations, confrontations and riots. And at least as important are supplemental channels such as letters to the editor, open microphone radio programs, community participation TV and videotape, and the like, insofar as these opinion forms stimulate feedback messages that later reach the government. (Guité, 1972)

Direct feedback is most likely analogous to "civic participation" in Almond and Verba's terms (Almond and Verba, 1965), which I would subsume under the rubric *determinative* feedback to mean participative political processes with a determinate end in mind, such as electing a party, gaining a new zoning regulation, etc. This I would contrast with *expressive* feedback, which would include the states of opinion over issues. Thus, polls and surveys and even letters would fall under the *expressive* rubric where instrumental means toward a specific objective are not used.

The public opinion poll is the most accepted method today by which governments, corporations, and other institutions in our society gain information on an opinion state. Thus, such polls *express* an existent attitude state. In North America, members of parliament and congressmen often poll their constituency to glean some notion of their opinions on leading social issues. As one congressman put it, "I believe it is an important part of the job of a congressman today to communicate with his constituents – and to assure that this communication is a two-way street." (Cleveland, 1972)

Polls, however, for a number of reasons, are not a sufficient answer to the need for feedback mechanisms; they are, in fact, quite limited in their ability to produce truly relevant feedback. Bauer has pointed out that the use of surveys as a social indicator is limited because their tendency to provide aggregate data "hides some phenomena of interest" (Bauer, 1967: 191), and Schiller has argued that they have "fostered the illusion of popular participation and freedom of choice to conceal an increasingly elaborate apparatus of conscious manipulation and mind management" (Schiller, 1971). Public opinion polls are, by their expressive nature, then, confined to functioning as reaction to a stimulus provided by the authorities – the sponsors of the poll (by some previous policy or act) and/or the poll takers, by the way in which they frame questions. Given the limited *universe of concern* of the sponsors, the reaction itself is not likely to be a reflection of a *population's* true universe of concerns any more than television ratings reflect anything beyond the state of preferences toward what is at that time available on television. There are, therefore, needs for feedback which in fact fall outside the limited universe of the poll taker and his sponsor and there are modes available now, which will be discussed later since they are the subject of this book and, in addition, there are channels made possible by the present state of our communications technology.

Another distinction that should be noted with reference to the term feedback is that used by Stevens in his study of Puerto Rico. Stevens distinguishes between "service feedback," e.g., requests for public services, inquiries for public information, and personal complaints; and "involvement feedback," e.g., more general opinions, suggestions for policy, and the volunteering of persons for more direct involvement in public issues (Stevens, 1970). It is interesting to note that 90 percent of the inquiries in the Puerto Rican feedback system directed by Stevens were of the service kind and only 10 percent were of the involvement type. The latter, by the way, would be analogous to public opinion and to the kinds of materials found in newspaper letter columns, but which are not necessarily expressive in nature. It is also noteworthy that feedback mechanisms of the kind Stevens writes about tend to bring together such phenomena as complaints, opinions, and information seeking under one umbrella; thus there is an empirical, if not analytic, relationship between these kinds of uses; and this suggests that the institutions we shall be exploring later in the book in a distinct sense share attributes of each other.

Going beyond the notion of the conceptual relationship between manifestly different uses of feedback, we also find a way in which the structure of feedback can be used to differentiate different social systems. Boulding suggests, for example, that in the *authoritarian* political system, decisions "originate with the higher roles and are transmitted to the lower roles as orders," while *information* is "transmitted from lower roles to higher roles on request of the higher role." This is feedback following the implementation of decisions from the top. "In the authoritarian model, the feedback is governed from above, not from below. It is not volunteered, it is requested. . . In the authoritarian model, the feedback is indirect and is to a considerable extent under the control of the higher roles themselves. In the democratic model, the feedback is much more direct and has a more powerful influence in the modification of decisions" (Boulding, 1971: 99-100). The latter corresponds fairly closely to my term *determinative* and the former term, although it has some cognitive overtones, nevertheless should be seen as expressive.

Although Boulding's model provides us with an interesting theoretical distinction that enables us to classify systems on a continuum ranging from democratic to totalitarian, nevertheless it obscures an important problem, to wit, the feedback difficulties which are not purposely built into the system in democratic societies whose manifest ideologies suggest the promotion of feedback but which in practice make it difficult or even nearly impossible:

In terms of effective information transmitted per unit time, none of the presently available channels of citizen feedback rivals the flow from the centers of power outward to the citizens via television and the press. . . . One result of such unidirectional communication is the increasing alienation of the citizen from political and social processes. (Umpleby, 1972: 66)

Thus, in a fully developed democracy with the maximum of technological channels of communication, the effective use of public opinion not to mention other forms of feedback becomes choked through the sheer weight of the difficulty of trying to make oneself heard; and when this happens, the area of unchallenged administrative decision making expands even under the mantle of a "participatory democracy."

Therefore, *actual* participation becomes the critical issue; and actual participation is not synomymous with *potential* access to channels, for access per se tells us nothing about the difficulties of the process itself for individuals differentially located in the social system. Perhaps the best example of this point is newspaper letter columns. On the surface they are available to all, but in practice only those who have been trained and practiced in literate feedback, meaning the better educated, are likely to commence the task of putting together a coherent letter to the editor. The contemporary concern over the ability of our schools to educate individuals so that they are competent in reading and writing has lately come under critical scrutiny and the million dollar suit by a Californian charging he was functionally illiterate upon graduation from high school is another piece of evidence in this regard. The telephone appears to be a workable instrument for person-to-person communication, one which does not require literacy, yet for many it is a difficult instrument to use and with which to gain results. A group of university students in London, Canada, experimenting with telephone usage to reach people who were important to their objectives, finally concluded that the telephone was not an effective instrument for communicating *upward* in our society (Singer, 1970).

Earlier I stressed the use of feedback as an instrument of opinion, i.e., its expressive function. However, Stevens' conceptual distinction between service and participatory uses adumbrated an area of concern that looms much larger and to which I alluded in the very beginning of this chapter; and that is its use as a means of carrying out *determinative* concerns. These concerns, rather than being ones that involve some group goal or beyond that some national goal, are in fact highly individual. They may be concerns that involve Square One: how to get basic information; or Square Two, the help which is an ultimate objective. Or the individual may have a complaint about a corporate or governmental bureau which he has not been able to satisfy. Furthermore, some feedback channels may have as inherent characteristics knowledge; others may not only have knowledge which is available but also trained personnel who help put it into action through an ombudsman function; still others may possess both of these factors to some degree but also possess the power to publicize a given case; the latter inevitably are mass media.

One of the reasons for heightened interest in this kind of feedback channel is that the pace of change is faster today. If feedback channels are not up to servicing individuals qua individuals during abrupt transformative periods, then individuals who are disoriented, like those who may wish to transmit an opinion about a social state, tend to move from the individual mode to the collective mode in order to achieve their objectives. The collective movements generated by the late Saul Alinksy were possible because of the failure of persons attempting to cope as individuals. In the same sense, I would agree with the authorities who describe such collective behavior as riots as communication. As the social landscape changes rapidly, information is more essential for the coping process; yet, decisions made at the uppermost levels of society filter down slowly, if at all; and oftentimes inaccurately, but importantly, some is lost in concatenations of other information. Changes in hospital insurance plans and federal tax provisions are obvious, ready, and substantial kinds of examples; telephone numbers and bureau auspices change overnight and individuals are confused, as if in a Kafkan nightmare concerning where to go, what bureau is responsible for a given problem, how one makes contact. Facts such as these have been documented in the United States by Kahn, who has pointed out that substantial numbers of people do not know how to find out about services which are available to them; in fact, the greater the needs of individuals, according to Kahn, the lower their access to relevant information (Kahn, 1966: 46, 60, 108).

In part this is, in fact, a function of the fact that knowledge is differentially found within different sections of the social system: the poor, typically, live in a more restricted information environment. But there are two other reasons as well. One is that values are in a heightened state of change; some have called the value change situation explosive, with well-established patterns dealing with family life, sex, occupations, and drugs being turned upside down and creating new information needs; one need only point out changed values concerning premarital sex and the technological information now desired by both the married and unmarried as one example. Information on new occupations created by technological change is another example. It was only a few short years ago that the term computer programmer would have been a strange one to the majority of university students. And this would be true for the nomenclature of drugs as well. Secondly, apart from values creating new styles of life from which ensues a need for knowledge, there is the sheer fact that 90 percent of all knowledge in existence has been generated during the lifetime of the individual, according to Toffler. From this flows two problems: the capacity of the individual to absorb the mass of new knowledge in any case, and the ability of our present information systems (i.e., the schools, the mass media, etc.) to be ready to present it, for the lead time required is too long to prepare new knowledge for when it is needed.

These problems, then, suggest the need in our rapidly changing society to assess the state of information institutions and the patterns of usage if we are to successfully plan to cope with change as a social system that desires to be responsive to the needs of individuals. We are thus led to ask what sources are *potentially* available; and such an inventory would include interpersonal networks of friends, the mass media, experts such as lawyers and physicians, bureaus, both governmental and corporate, libraries, information centers, elected representatives, and educational insitutions, among the leading ones. The means would include personal visits, telephone calls and letters (all of which are *demand* modes) and unscheduled or *nondemand* modes such as mass media announcements as well as mailed and telephoned unscheduled information. In addition to recognizing their presence, it is important to learn how truly accessible these sources and modes are to different groups in terms of need and ability to find and use them. Detailed investigation of present usage patterns of each of the sources would aid us in understanding not only how present institutions function today and for whom, but will also aid us in envisioning new feedback institutions suited to the needs of our society and the groups within it that will use them; beyond this, such analysis will aid us in understanding the categories of need and thus will function as another important social indicator, one not subject to the constraints of traditional survey and poll techniques.

It was in the context of this concern that the studies upon which the present book is based were generated; for an opportunity presented itself to conduct three separate researches concerned with feedback, each of a mass character and all, advantageously, during the same approximate period of time and in the same community. Prior to examining the findings, past research bearing on similar kinds of feedback will be presented and discussed.

In the next chapter, research bearing on letter writing, phone-in radio shows, the newspaper ombudsman, and information centers will be surveyed.

References

Almond, Gabriel A., and Verba, Sidney. *The Civic Culture.* Boston: Little, Brown and Co., 1965.

Bauer, Raymond A. "Societal Feedback." *Annals of the American Academy,* Vol. 373 (September 1967), 180-92.

Boulding, Kenneth E. *The Image.* Ann Arbor: University of Michigan Press, 1971.

Cleveland, James C. Speech in House of Representatives. *Congressional Record.* September 27, 1972.

Guité, Michael. *Ottawa.* Department of Communication, unpublished paper, 1972.

Kahn, Alfred J. *Neighborhood Information Centers.* New York: Columbia University School of Social Work, 1966.

Kitto, H.D.F. *The Greeks.* Baltimore: Penguin Books, 1956.

Meier, Richard L. *A Communications Theory of Urban Growth.* Cambridge: M.I.T. Press, 1962.

Schiller, Herbert I. "The Polling Industry: The Measurement and Manufacture of Opinion." Paper presented to the Society for the History of Technology Annual Meeting, 1971.

Singer, Benjamin D. "Access to Information: A Position Paper on Communication Channels and Social Change." Presented to the Telecommunication Meetings on Access to Information, 1970.

Stevens, Chandler H. *A Moderate Proposal.* Unpublished paper, 1972.

_____ . "Science, Government and Citizen Feedback." *Operations Research* 18, 4 (July-August 1970).

Toffler, Alvin. *Future Shock.* New York: Random House, 1970.

Umpleby, Stewart A. "Is Greater Citizen Participation in Planning Possible and Desirable?" *Technological Forecasting and Social Change* 4 (1972), 61-76.

Wiener, Norbert. *The Human Use of Human Beings.* Boston: Houghton Mifflin, 1964.

2

Research Into Mass Feedback

There is little research dealing with feedback in written and printed media. And that which exists is of limited value for a number of reasons, including the research objectives and the methods by which these objectives were sought.

One of the early studies (Sayre, 1939) describes research which analyzed letters written by listeners to an American radio show of the 1930s, "America's Town Meeting of the Air," in which an attempt was made to estimate the social status of the sender by such surface criteria as quality of paper, cleanliness, punctuation and spelling, words and phrases used, etc. The results of this primitive "content analysis" were not reported, but in any case the validity of such a method is highly questionable for a multiplicity of reasons. However, the postmarks were a valid indicator of the kinds of areas from which the letters were sent, even if the surface criteria did not make it possible to really identify the balance of the sociological identity of the senders. The writers of letters were located in larger cities, with cities of 100,000 and more over-represented by 60 percent and towns of less than 2,500 under-represented by 75 percent (Sayre: 275). This fact alone suggests that access to and/or use of feedback channels are related to factors commonly studied by sociologists.

In perhaps the best analysis to date of letter writing to public officials, Leila Sussmann (1959) traces the pattern in the United States beginning with the first two decades of the nineteenth century when "only a narrow elite engaged in this type of letter writing," to the 1950s when congressional and presidential assistants were assigned to read and to compile statistical summaries of letters mounting to the millions (Sussmann: 203) During Lincoln's tenure, the mail count (at the time of the Civil War) reached a rate of 44 per 10,000 literate adults and by Franklin D. Roosevelt's time, during the depression, it had soared to 160 (Sussmann: 204). National emergencies such as was and depressions increase the mail flow. Sussman found that the principal factor in the increased mail flow could be traced to advances in the general educational level:

A certain minimum facility with language and pen is prerequisite for writing a letter. Education is also linked to *political* letter writing through the intervening variable of political interest. Well educated people are known to be more interested in politics than the less educated, and political interest is highly related to political letter writing (Sussmann: 205)

Almond and Verba's study of five nations. (1965: 163-65) confirms the relationship between education and the sense of political efficacy.

9

Among other factors, Sussmann includes the development of mass communications media, particularly radio, which through its ability to generate constant interest in national and international news also encouraged political mail (Sussmann: 205). Father Coughlin, for example, is said to have received 1,200,00 letters in response to one broadcast in 1930 (Sussmann: 211). Overall, Sussmann estimates that from 15 to 20 percent of the American electorate have written a *political* letter to some public official at some time in their lives (Sussmann: 206).

A more recent study of letter writing examined letters from citizens of Wisconsin addressed to certain of the state's administrative offices and found that the largest number of letters complained of a lack of response to an early communication to an administrative agency (Olson: 1969).

The little research that has been done on letters as feedback to officials has focused upon letter writing as a political mechanism on the one hand, in which an individual presents his opinion on an issue to an official, and as a request for information or help on the other. There are, of course, other channels that can be used to reach individuals directly, including personal visits, confrontations, and the telephone. There is no data available at this time on these modes of feedback.

Letters to Newspapers

There is considerably more research available dealing with letters to the editors of newspapers. Its weakness lies in the fact that this research, for the most part, consists of counts of letters to newspapers, surveys of writers of published letters, and content analysis of such letters. As Grey and Brown point out:

since most of the 30 years research on letters-to-the-editor has been based on only those published, it may be that the profile which has emerged reflects less the writers themselves than the selection of editors. A broader but largely invisible cross section of Americans may have been writing for some time; theirs may be the inarticulate, sometimes abusive letters screened from print. Until more systematic knowledge of editorial selection decisions is available, we may be losing valuable indicators of political attitudes, frustrations and change. (Grey and Brown: 471)

In spite of the limitations indicated above, we shall review the research that has been done to date on letter writing to newspapers for the insights that may be provided.

Probably the two most prestigious newspapers (from the point of view of having a letter published) in North America are *The New York Times* and the *Toronto Globe and Mail*. In the case of *The New York Times,* which published its first letter several days after its first issue appeared on September 18, 1851, approximately 40,000 letters are received per year, 4.4 for each 100 papers sold (based on 40,000 letters and 902,437 circulation).[a] The *Globe and Mail,* with a circulation of 287,621, receives approximately 10,000 letters for a ratio of 3.5 per 100 papers sold. The *London Free Press,* data for which are analyzed later in this report, has a total circulation of 119,340 and receives 2,100 letters per year for a ratio of 1.8 letters per 100 papers sold daily. The probability of letters being published is 6 percent for *The New York Times,* 36 percent for the *Globe and Mail,* and 80 percent for the *London Free Press.* The probability is in part related to the *circulation* of the newspaper, obviously, but is also related to the number *sent* per 100 readers. That *New York Times* readers are more likely to write than readers of the *London Free Press* probably reflects the fact that its aduience is more articulate, of higher social status, and more involved in national and world affairs.

Some evidence that one's social status is associated with the likelihood of writing to newspapers comes from studies that have been done primarily of letter writers themselves. Vacin (1965) found in a study of 123 letter writers to three Kansas daily newspapers that letter writers were higher than average in terms of education and of occupational status and subscribed to an average of four magazines. Forsythe (1950) studied forty-four letter writers in Kentucky and reported that they were predominantly middle aged and older (median age was 59), above average in education and occupation, possessed an essentially "local" orientation, and were conservative in their world views. The content of the letters column of the *Times* of London, England, is described as "an authentic . . . expression of the upper-middle class. . . . A few thousand well-placed men and women, who instinctively know each other's feelings, signal to each other in print" (Lewis, 1970: 54). One individual who attempted to compile the professions of published writers in the *Times* of London, England, submitted this list: (Lewis: 62)

Dons and Schoolmasters		436
MPs	Conservative	147
	Socialist	138
	Liberal	7
	Other	10

The New York Times has been accused of favoring big names: "Some names that have graced the letters column in recent years include three men who later became President: Kennedy, Johnson, and Nixon; also Hubert Humphrey, Dean Acheson, Robert Kennedy, John Kenneth Galbraith, Felix Frankfurter, Prince

---

[a]The circulation figure is based upon the current data for the average number of weekday, Saturday and Sunday papers sold.

Sihanouk of Cambodia, Jean-Paul Sartre, Martin Luther King, Helen Keller, William Faulkner . . ." (Rosenthal, 1969: 116).

It is also clear that letter counts per se may give misleading indications of how widespread letter writing is, for there are some non-celebrity writers who appear repeatedly and who are described as "professional" letter writers. Charles Hooper, who was active earlier in the century and who had had published sixteen letters in *The New York Times* by 1936, prior to its establishment of a two per person per year limit, had written by his own estimate hundreds of thousands of letters to newspapers before his death in 1941 (Rosenthal: 116). Marvin Wolfson, a Brooklyn economics teacher, credited with being the "most prolific and persistent writer of letters to the (N.Y.) *Times*" has had 2,000 letters published in various places since 1927 (Rosenthal: 116). According to *Newsweek,* one individual, Alan Kline, has written 3,000 letters in nine years, of which 1,500 were published (*Newsweek,* Jan. 2, 1961: 48).

There is some evidence that suggests, on one hand, limited participation by the great mass of individuals and on the other, rising interest and participation and a possible shift in the sociological characteristics of the contemporary letter writer. A survey done by the Michigan Survey Research Center of the 1964 U.S. presidential campaign found that only 3 percent of the electorate had ever "written a politically relevant letter to the editor of a newspaper or magazine" (Grey and Brown: 454). Yet, according to Rosenau (cited in Grey and Brown: 456), there is a "small, but nonetheless steady, expansion in the number of citizens who develop and maintain a continuing interest in public affairs" and as proof that such is growing faster than the population, Rosenau cites data that suggests a "surge of letter writing activity in the 1960's" (Grey and Brown: 471). *The New York Times'* increase in letters received between 1958 to 1966 was 12 percent per year as daily circulation increased 1.6 percent annually; the circulation of the *New York Post* decreased between 1955 and 1966, at the same time as its mail was increasing more than 5 percent annually. This was found true for other newspapers in the East, Midwest and West (Grey and Brown: 471). Similar findings for the last few years are found in an unpublished study by Singer and Cameron for Canadian daily newspapers (1971). Larry Smith, editor in chief of the *St. Catherines Standard,* reported that "in the past year we have seen a tremendous increase in letters received and used." The *Orillia Packet and Times* reported, "We are getting more letters now than ever before." The *Stratford Beacon Herald* said the "number of letters received has increased substantially in the past year or so." The now defunct *Telegram* also reported a "greater volume of mail coming in."

The question dealing with why some people participate by writing is not the same as what stimulated them to write. Some analysts point to needs of the individual and others stress factors external to the individual. However, one theme that recurs revolves around the *catharsis* function in one form or another. Leo Bogart, in his analysis of fan mail, suggests as motives "The general 'excitability' of the person; his psychological need to express himself; the importance he assigns to his letter – that is, the things he expects it to accomplish" (Bogart: 434).

Wyant and Herzog, in their analysis of interviews conducted with sixty-five people who wrote to their senators in 1940 concerning a selective service bill, classified the motives of writers as either "expressive" or "instrumental."[b] The instrumental writers sought to influence the passage of the bill and the expressive individuals appeared more concerned with the gratification they received from writing per se, the feeling that they were performing a duty as a conscientious citizen (Sussmann: 207).

Forsythe asserted that newspaper letter writers reported to him that "they describe themselves as crusaders for this or that special cause, some stating that letter writing is a means for 'blowing off steam,' " and concludes that letter columns function as a "social safety valve" (Forsythe: 144). Vacin (1965) suggests in his survey of newspaper letter writers that writers were convinced that they were in some way or another affecting events through their letters. Lewis, on the other hand, has described the function of the London *Times* letter columns as gossip among insiders (Lewis: 144).

Davis and Rarick's study of editorials and letters to the editor in 1962 in Oregon newspapers, in which the subject of discussion was whether a communist should be allowed to speak at state supported colleges and universities, indicated that "examination of the letters revealed frequent references to editorials and to other letters. Consequently, it appears that the editorials often stimulated letter writers and that letters in turn often stimulated further letter writers" (Davis and Rarick: 109). The content analysis by Grey and Brown of California newspapers during the 1968 U.S. presidential campaign also agreed that "many letters were triggered by an editorial or some other letter. Although some volunteered their thoughts, most people simply responded to something they had read in the paper" (Grey and Brown: 454). They cite a study conducted nearly a third of a century earlier than theirs (Foster and Friedrich, cited in Grey and Brown: 453), which found:

1. The newspaper itself conveyed the most frequent stimulus to write to the editor. The majority of published letters referred to news items, other letters or to editorials.
2. Most letters are 'agin' something or somebody.

The answer to why this form of participation is increasing may be related in great part, as Sussmann asserted, to social structural changes, such as a higher

---

[b]My own use of "expressive" earlier differs in that it is meant as a descriptive state rather than as a personal motive.

proportion of educated, literate people as well as the increase in proportions of young people.

In addition, a further explanation for the rising participation in printed forums may be the shift from passivity to activism of younger people (as well as minorities) who in the past were not heard as often, along with the earlier mentioned rise in educational levels. Young people or individuals represented as leaders in youth cults are shown in the mass media asserting themselves, making demands, being interviewed; they may serve as role models and stimuli for others to assert themselves in the public media (Singer, 1972). Alvin Toffler (*Future Shock,* 1970: 274) quotes a letter by Allen Ginsberg to Timothy Leary:

Yesterday got on TV with N. Mailer and Ashley Montagu and gave big speech . . . recommending everybody get high . . . Got in tough with all the liberal pro-dope people I know to have [a certain pro-drug report] publicized and circulated. . . . I wrote a five-page summary of the situation to this friend Kenny Love on the *New York Times* and he said he'd perhaps do a story (newswise) . . . which could then be picked up by U.P. friend on national wire. Also gave copy to Al Aronowitz on *New York Post* and Rosalind Constable at *Time* and Bob Silvers on *Harper's* . . .

As to what stimulates individuals to write who might not otherwise, Sussmann's insightful comment concerning radio can be extended to television: more issues and more controversial issues are presented than ever before, resulting in greater consciousness and stimulation for more people. Radio and television forums, rather than replacing the printed columns, may well be stimulating greater use of them.

Thus, the interaction of social structural forces, social psychological effects (the aforementioned role modeling), technological developments (television and the call-in show), and perhaps even the media ombudsman, a new social invention, undoubtedly are interacting to explain the surge in participation in the printed media.

The Newspaper Ombudsman

The Newspaper ombudsman is a new social invention that answers in part the question posed by William F. Buckley in an article entitled "Why Don't We Complain?" Buckley says that the reason people in America do not complain is

because we are all increasingly anxious in America to be unobtrusive, we are reluctant to make our voices heard, hesitant about claiming our rights; we are afraid that our cause is unjust, or that if it is not unjust, that it is ambiguous; or if not even that, that it is too trivial to justify the horrors of a confrontation with Authority . . .(Buckley, *Esquire,* Jan. 1971: 48)

The newspaper ombudsman goes by many names. In Detroit, in the *Detroit Free Press,* the column is called "Action Line." In London, Ontario, the column is called "Sound Off." The principle is always the same: people who cannot solve their problems call, write, or appear in person to complain about red tape, consumer frauds, non-response from government officials or corporations. Armed with the power of publicity, along with experience in handling similar cases, the newspaper ombudsman solves the problem in a majority of cases. The idea apparently originated with Bill Steven, editor of the *Houston Chronicle,* who initiated the ombudsman column "Watchem" in 1961 (*Time,* Feb. 3, 1967: 58). Since then, it has become an institution found in increasing numbers of North American newspapers, and in many newspapers it is the best read column.

It is uncertain whether the newspaper ombudsman exists because of the inability of people to find other effective means to complain by which they may solve their own problems or whether the existence of the newspaper ombudsman is in fact proof that people do complain, despite Mr. Buckley's assertion to the contrary. There has been no published social scientific research into this new institution to date apart from that presented later in this book and a recently completed master's thesis done by a student of the author (Hannigan, 1972). There will be further reference to the media ombudsman function as well in the section dealing with electronic media.

The Radio Call-In Show

The radio phone-in show is a synthesis of two electronic means of communications, the telephone (wired medium) and the radio (wireless), whose roots are found in the early telephone quiz shows of the 1930s when quiz show moderators telephoned members of the population to ask them questions which, if correctly answered, resulted in prizes. Later technical developments made it possible to conveniently broadcast the respondent's end of the conversation and a delay mechanism then made it possible to control messages from the audience.

By the late 1940s, at about the time that television was preparing to usurp some of radio's network function and help transform it into an essentially localized medium, early programs of this nature began to appear; but it was not until the early 1960s that call-in programming began in earnest. Today, few major population centers in North America do not have their version of the phone-in radio show. This social invention, which facilitates feedback from the audience, has now become a communications institution through its ubiquity.

To date, however – although it is ubiquitous – there has been no systematic research into it which would make it possible to understand what role it plays in modern communication systems in society. Even if it is not now considered to be an important part of mass communications systems, perhaps it could play a more significant role in the future as a medium for individuals to express their opinions, to secure information, to get help, or to gain psychological benefits through participating in the larger social and political processes.

As scattered and poor as the research into written and printed feedback is, it still exceeds in both quantity and quality the research to date on feedback through the electronic media. Most of what has been done has been impressionistic and found in popular magazines, with the exception of a recent article by Crittenden in *The Public Opinion Quarterly* (1971), of limited scope and even more limited validity.

Newsweek (March 30, 1964: 74) traces the history of the radio talk show back to the late '40s in the United States, but another source suggests that the "all-talk trend" was initiated by radio station KABC in Los Angeles in 1963 (McEachern, *Today's Health,* July 1970: 69). In any case, this social invention swept to great heights of popularity in most North American cities during the 1960s and remains unabated today. Some reasons that have been offered for the great willingness of people to participate include anonymity, the fact that it is easier to talk than write, the sensational topics that are exposed, their gossipy nature, the fact that the shows are a return to the small-town forum amidst the forces of mass society that make our lives mechanistic and cut us off from the primary groups we need for sustenance. However, there has been another function that most programs perform and some have come to specialize in: that of the electronic ombudsman. This they share with the other social invention of mass media that has swept to great popularity during the 1960s, the newspaper ombudsman.

The electronic media's feedback operations seem to share the major attributes of the two printed media already mentioned, letters to the editor and the newspaper ombudsman: an opportunity to present one's opinion on some topic (letters to the editor) or an opportunity to get help for a complaint or information.

A recent article by Crittenden (*The Public Opinion Quarterly,* 1971: 200) addresses itself essentially to the first function. The study was based on a mail survey with a 56 percent return (of random selections from the phone directory) in Terre Haute, Indiana, in 1967; interviews with regular callers and questionnaires sent to local leaders. The validity of the research with respect to callers is dubious, for the sample return provided only eleven persons who said they had ever called the "Speak Out" show; nine of the eleven were female. The survey essentially attempted to tap interest in the show by listeners.

The survey indicated that of the 111 usable returns of individuals (out of a target population of 200), 46 percent had listened to the program one or more times during the past four weeks and 47 percent of the respondents indicated some interest or a great deal of interest in the program.

The content analysis portion of the research also suffers from the fact that the sample was quite limited (169 message units) and done during the summer only. Coding was by topic (content) rather than form or purpose except for a brief statement dealing with the interaction form "opposition, support or ambiguous or irrelevant" (Crittenden: 207). The content analysis indicated the following frequencies:

Government services and policies	45
Community controversies	38
Private, individual or group behavior	32
The flag	21
Chit chat (personal conversations, reminiscence, requests for information)	14
International affairs	9
Comments on program	6
Unclassifiable or unknown	4
	169

Ignored was the notion of any stimulus to call contained on the show unless one makes the assumption that all 169 message units were stimulated by the program alone rather than there having been a self-initiating process as well (these issues will be discussed later in the present report). Crittenden's coding scheme ignores the important ombudsman function of call-in radio shows as well as of its information function by collapsing such elements in the categories as "private individual or group behavior" and "chit chat" (Crittenden: 204).

Moving on to the ombudsman function of two-way radio, probably the most unique demonstration of the ombudsman function as it is carried out in broadcasting, melds the two-way operation of telephone with the power of broadcasting to publicize local community problems that call for action. In fact, that is the name of the most effective radio ombudsman North America has seen, "Call for Action." The concept was pioneered by New York radio station WMCA in 1963. The station included it in its regular format of pop music, disc jockeys, and news. The station began to invite complaints from individuals about their problems, such as garbage removal, rat and pest control, voter registration, consumer fraud, air and water pollution, taxes and tax information, etc. A staff of volunteers, equipped with an ever-growing list of sources of information "that could be used to solve problems once they were properly delineated," manned the telephones. In three years, 45,000 complaints poured in. If the complainant was not satisfied, the volunteers contacted the agency, landlord, etc., with the implicit and often explicit threat of exposing the problem on radio. Where there was no response or insufficient response, the radio station broadcast a series of strong editorials (see Appendix) which most often produced the meliorative efforts desired. Ultimately, the idea was successfully adopted in Washington,

D.C., by radio station WWDC as well. The importance of this kind of channel for initiating action "from the top" is expressed by Nicholas Johnson, Federal Communications Commissioner: "It seems to me that no governmental institution can link government to the people as well as can radio and television. And broadcasting can become even more of a two-way means of communication which allows the people to reach their government – and other people."[c]

Although "Call for Action" demonstrates the two-way ombudsman function of electronic media in the purest sense, the same function is being performed, along with others, in most of the call-in radio shows being broadcast today. And, indeed, as data to be presented later will show, such radio broadcasts may be performing a different mix of services for persons than is true for other feedback media.

The Information Center

The information center is a relatively new social invention. It is worth noting that as late as 1962 there was very little if any attention devoted to this institution. In Fritz Machlup's admirably comprehensive statistical survey monograph, *The Production and Distribution of Knowledge in the United States* (1962), there is no mention of such centers as one of the sources for dissemination of information. Nevertheless, by the 1970s community information centers in Canada were "springing up in so many communities . . . that it was almost impossible to keep track of them" (Stewart and Stars, 1972). However, Ironside has identified 159 information centers in Canada in 1971 (1972).

These centers had as their forebears the British Citizens Advice Bureaux, developed after the Second World War by social workers attempting to provide orientation to individuals "dislocated" as a result of the war, and Neighborhood Information Centers in the U.S.A., according to Helling (1971) and to Head (1971). The British institution provides information and advice on a broad range of general problems and government services; the American institution tends to move in the direction of greater involvement with the individual's problem, and advocacy. A dimension which distinguishes centers is the size of their catchment area, with neighborhood centers tending to provide more direct involvement by workers, and community centers tending to provide more of an information service.

The Canadian information centers' existence appears to be a response to a pressing documented need for more and better information; as the Report of the Task Force on Government Information indicated, there are great areas of ignorance among programs and the desire was expressed, particularly by lower

---

[c]WMCA Radio Station brochure, "Call for Action" (n.d.).

socioeconomic groups, for more information.[d] Yet, more and more of the information needed by individuals is either hidden in record files or within the social-bureaucratic confines of organizations. Peter Drucker (1971: 171) has pointed out, "Historians two hundred years hence may see as central to the twentieth century what we ourselves have been paying almost no attention to: the emergence of a society of organizations in which every single social task of importance is entrusted to a large institution." It is an interesting commentary on our age to point to the development of organizations which in great part communicate with other organizations on behalf of individuals.

References

Almond, Gabriel A., and Verba, Sidney. *The Civic Culture.* Boston: Little, Brown and Co., 1965.

Bauer, Raymond A. "Societa Feedback." *Annals Amer. Acad. Political and Social Sciences,* Vol. 373 (September 1967), 180-92.

"Beeping Toms." *Newsweek,* Vol. 63 (March 30, 1964), 74.

Bogart, Leo. "Fan Mail for the Philharmonic." *Public Opinion Quarterly* (Fall 1949), 423-24.

Boulding, Kenneth E. *The Image.* Ann Arbor: University of Michigan Press, 1971.

Buckley, William F. "Why Don't We Complain?" *Esquire* (January 1971), 47-48.

Crittenden, John. "Democratic Functions of the Open Mike Radio Forum." *Public Opinion Quarterly* (Summer 1971), 200-210.

Davis, Maj. Hal, and Rarick, Galen. "Functions of Editorials and Letters to the Editor." *Journalism Quarterly,* Vol. 41 (1964), 108-109.

Drucker, Peter F. *The Age of Discontinuity.* New York: Harper and Row, 1969.

Forsythe, Sidney A. "An Exploratory Study of Letters to the Editor and Their Contributors." *Public Opinion Quarterly* (Spring 1950), 143-44.

Grey, David L., and Brown, Trevor R. "Letters to the Editor: Hazy Reflections of Public Opinion." *Journalism Quarterly,* Vol. 47 (Autumn 1970), 450-56, 471.

Hannigan, John A. "The Newspaper Ombudsman and the Redress of Consumer Complaints." Master's thesis, University of Western Ontario, 1972.

Head, Wilson A. *Partners in Information.* Queen's Part: 1971.

Helling, R.A. "An Appraisal of the Community Information Centre Study Project." Windsor: March 1, 1971.

---

[d]Task Force on Government Information, *To Know and Be Known* (Ottawa: Queen's Printer, 1969).

Ironside, Diana J., and Associates. *The Power to Communicate.* Ottawa: Consumers' Association of Canada, 1972.

Kahn, Alfred J. *Neighborhood Information Centers.* New York: Columbia University School of Social Work, 1966.

Lewis, Anthony. "The Jungle Drum of the British Establishment." *Esquire,* Vol. 74 (November 1970), 52, 54, 56, 58, 62, 64.

McEachern, Margaret. "The Town Meeting Is Not Dead — It's Alive and Well on Radio." *Today's Health* (July 1970), 32-33, 69-71.

Machlup, Fritz. *The Production and Distribution of Knowledge in the United States.* Princeton: Princeton University Press, 1962.

"Not Just Words — But Action." *Time,* Vol. 89 (February 3, 1967), 58.

Olson, David J. "Citizen Grievance Letters as a Gubernatiorial Control Device in Wisconsin." *Journal of Poltics,* Vol. 31 (August 1969), 741-55.

Rosenthal, Irving. "Who Writes the 'Letters to the Editor'?" *Saturday Review* (September 13, 1969), 114-16.

Sayre, Jeanette. "Progress in Radio Fan-Mail Analysis." Reprinted from Research Activities. Edited by Hadley Cantril. *Public Opinion Quarterly* (April 1939), 272-78.

Singer, Benjamin D. "Mass Society, Mass Media and the Transformation of Minority Identity." *British Journal of Sociology* (in press).

_____ . "Access to Information: A Position Paper on Communication Channels and Social Change." Presented at the Telecommunications Seminar, Department of Communications, Ottawa, May 16, 1970.

Singer, Benjamin D., and Cameron, Andrew D. "Letters to the Editor." An unpublished study, 1971.

_____ . "The Radio Call-In Show." An unpublished study, 1972.

Stewart, Gail, and Stars, Cathy. "The Community Information Network Proposal." *Canadian Consumer* (January-February 1972).

Sussmann, Leila. "Mass Political Letter Writing in America: The Growth of An Institution." *Public Opinion Quarterly,* Vol. 23 (1959), 203-212.

"Taking Pen in Hand." *Newsweek,* Vol. 57 (January 2, 1961), 48.

Task Force on Government Information. *To Know and Be Known.* Ottawa: Queen's Printer, 1969.

Toffler, Alvin C. *Future Shock.* New York: Random House, 1970.

Vacin, Gary L. "A Study of Letter Writers." *Journalism Quarterly,* Vol. 42 (Summer 1965), 464-66.

3 Toward an Analysis of Mass Feedback Channels: The Questions and the Methods

The study of mass feedback channels, as is evident from the literature reviewed, is insufficient to the task. I propose to contribute toward a solution of this problem, first of all, by attempting to identify the *mass* channels that may be available in a typical North American city that make it possible for individuals to participate in the process of opinion formation; to inquire, to seek help. It will be recalled that a number of sources of different types were listed near the end of Chapter 1 and that mass channels were among the many sources suggested which now exist. Perhaps the most general question will be devoted to finding out something about present usages, i.e., what proportion of the population uses each of the major channels at present.

In addition, we shall want to know who has access to such channels, *who* meaning the sociological identity of the users. There is no sociological profile available other than the very selective and dated information of the limited past research reviewed in the last chapter, e.g., the description of the social characteristics of newspaper letter writers which leads us to believe these participants are quite elderly. Again, the highly "visible" voices of extremists we hear on the typical call-in radio show leads us to develop a pronounced stereotype of the typical user from which we make inferences about the very usefulness of this kind of channel in society.

Furthermore, we shall want to know how the various channels, printed and electronic, compare in carrying out relevant social functions, and what kinds of functions they are performing. This kind of information is valuable in assessing the present state of feedback institutions and in permitting us, therefore, to work toward modeling new social inventions made possible by the present availability of communications technologies, as well as providing a sociological portrait of contemporary institutions.

The methods by which such analysis will be undertaken involves a multiple research thrust. The major research is based on a sample survey of the population of London, Ontario. This was carried out near the end of 1970 and will help to provide population parameters: the frequency and forms of usage of the mass media channels. An adjunct research consists of a content analysis of several thousand telephone calls taped from the broadcasts of call-in radio shows during 1970 and 1971. Finally, there is an analysis made during the second half of 1971, of clients of an information center in London. Fortunately, all three researches were done in the same city over the same approximate period of time;

so, whatever data have been provided permit the reader to make a more valid comparison of the different institutions with little concern that the differences were a product, essentially, of time and place. What follows will be a description of the methodologies and samples of each of the three studies.

The Sample Survey: Methodology and Description of Sample

The primary source of data for this report consists of the results of a large sample survey ($N = 1,000$) of adults, conducted in London, Ontario, in November and December 1970.[a]

The interview guide included questions dealing with "participatory media," i.e., use of letters to the editor, the "Sound Off" column of the *London Free Press* and call-in radio shows. The questions relevant to the present report are reproduced in the Appendix.

The sampling frame used in this study was provided by the Municipal Tax Assessment Office, which made available 1970 tax assessment records for all dwelling units (commercial and noncommercial) within the incorporated limits of London. The records are filed by ward level (seven in all), each of which is further delineated by subdivision. The total number of subdivisions is 504, from which a random sample of 101 subdivisions was selected.

A total of 14,373 residential units existed among the 101 subdivisions upon removal of all commercial units. A systematic sample of 1 in 12 ($N = 1,196$) residential units was selected from this total. Of the 1,196 units chosen, 1,000 units were actually interviewed. No interviews were obtained from 196 residential units either because they were vacant, because the respondents in the unit refused, or because the interviewer failed to establish contact with the members in that unit.[b]

Socioeconomic Description of Sample

The demographic characteristics of the sample drawn in November and December 1970 parallel in important respects the London population as described in the Census of Canada. The Census of Canada of 1966 was used when available, supplemented by data from the Census of 1961. The sample consisted of 471 males and 529 females.

Age. With respect to age (as can be seen in table 3.1), the age category of 19 and

---

[a]The survey was conducted in cooperation with Professors C. Nobbe, G. Ebanks, J. Williams, R. Osborn, and M. Rokeach of the University of Western Ontario.
[b]This description of the sampling procedure was provided by the sampling director, Dr. C.E. Nobbe.

Table 3-1

Age of Respondents and 1966 London Census Age Breakdown by Sex (Percentage)

Age Category	Sample			1966 Census		
	Male %	Female %	Total %	Male %	Female %	Total %
15–19	0.9	2.9	1.9	12.5	12.0	12.2
20–24	17.6	17.8	17.7	11.0	12.0	11.6
25–29	17.6	11.2	14.2	10.1	9.4	9.7
30–34	9.6	8.6	9.1	9.5	8.7	9.1
35–39	8.3	12.3	10.4	10.1	9.2	9.6
40–44	8.1	8.0	8.0	10.1	9.6	9.9
45–49	8.1	10.0	9.1	8.5	8.0	8.2
50–54	7.6	6.6	7.1	7.5	6.9	7.1
55–59	7.2	6.8	7.0	5.9	5.8	5.9
60–64	3.9	3.1	3.5	4.6	4.9	4.7
65–69	3.9	3.7	3.8	3.5	4.2	3.9
70–74	3.3	3.7	3.5	3.0	3.7	3.4
75–79	2.6	3.3	3.0	1.9	2.8	2.4
80 and above	1.3	2.0	1.7	1.8	2.8	2.3
Total	100.0	100.0	100.0	100.0	100.0	100.0

Source: Dominion Bureau of Statistics, *1966 Census Population (General Characteristics)*, (Ottawa: Queen's Printer), Vol. 1, "Age Groups," pp. 23–25, Table 23: Population by Five Year Age Groups and Sex, 1966.
Note: *N* excludes 29 respondents (12 male and 17 female) who didn't give their age.

below is underrepresented in the sample. This was deliberate and resulted from the sampling procedure of excluding most respondents who were less than 19 years of age since the population of interest is the London adult population. The 20-24 and 25-29 age categories are overrepresented (17.7 percent and 14.2 percent sample representation in these respective categories as compared to 11.6 percent and 9.7 percent in these categories in the Census findings), but in other pertinent respects the distribution of the sample age categories corresponds fairly closely to those of the London Census age categories.

Nearly a third of the sample (33.8 percent) is under 30. Half of the sample is in the 30-60 age category (50.7 percent) and the remaining 15.5 percent are in the 60 and over category. A total of twenty-nine respondents refused to indicate their ages.

Marital Status. Table 3.2 indicates three-quarters (76.2 percent) of the people interviewed were married, one-seventh (13.4 percent) were single, and one-tenth (10.4 percent) were divorced, separated or widowed. The single category is underrepresented in the sample because of the greater difficulty of finding single respondents home after repeated call-backs.

Table 3–2
Marital Status of Respondents and 1966 London Census Marital Status Data (15 Years and Over)

	Sample			1966 Census		
	Male %	Female %	Combined %	Male %	Female %	Combined %
Single	12.5	14.2	13.4	26.8	23.6	25.2
Married	82.6	70.5	76.2	69.7	64.1	66.8
Widowed	3.0	11.2	7.3	2.9	11.2	7.2
Divorced	.6	1.5	1.1	.6	1.0	.8
Separated	1.3	2.7	2.0	not recorded	not recorded	not recorded
Total	100.0	100.0	100.0	100.0	99.9	100.0
	N = 471	N = 529	N = 1,000	N = 68,692	N = 75,586	N = 144, 273

Source: Dominion Bureau of Statistics, *1966 Census, Population (General Characteristics)*, (Ottawa: Queen's Printer), Vol. 1, "Marital Status by Age Groups and Sex," pp. 35–37, Table 35: Population 15 Years of Age and Over by Marital Status, 1966.

Table 3–3
Religion of Respondents Compared With 1961 Census Data

	Sample Percentage	*Population (1961) Percentage*
Protestant	65.7	72.9
Roman Catholic	20.2	19.5
Other–Christian	6.9	5.0
Jewish	0.6	0.7
Other–Non-Christian	0.6	(Not recorded)
None	5.8	(Not recorded)
No Response	0.2	(Not recorded)
Total	100.0	100.1
	N = 1,000	*N* = 181,283

Source: Derived from Dominion Bureau of Statistics, *1961 Census, Population (General Characteristics)*, (Ottawa: Queen's Printer, 1962), Vol. 1–Part 2, "Religious Denominations," pp. 45–47, Table 45: Population by Religious Denominations and Sex, 1961.

Religion. As can be seen in table 3.3, almost two-thirds (65.7 percent) of the people in the sample were Protestants compared with the Census figure of 72.9. One-fifth (20.2 percent) of the respondents were Catholic (Census figure: 19.5 percent), and .6 percent were of the Jewish faith (Census 0.7 percent). Over 5 percent of the people interviewed indicated that they had no religious affiliation, a category not included in the 1961 Census.

Education. In order to compare the educational characteristics of the sample population with the London population of the 1961 Census (see table 3.4), it was necessary to eliminate the effect of the population under 19 years of age from both the Census data and the sample. The sample population and the 1961 Census of London include both individuals over 19 years of age who are no longer attending school as well as those still going to school.

As seen in table 3.4, about one-sixth (17.7 percent) of the sample respondents had a primary school level of education or less compared to 34 percent of the people in the 1961 Census. A little over one-half (56.3 percent) of the people interviewed were high school graduates or had some high school education; the 1961 Census shows that 57.6 percent of London's over 19 population were high school graduates or had some high school education.

A quarter of the sample (26 percent) had some college education, were college graduates, or had undertaken some postgraduate training. The overrepresentation in the highly educated category compared with the 1961 Census data (8.1 percent), undoubtedly results from the significant increase in the proportion of individuals attending university in 1970 compared with the

Table 3–4

Education Level of Respondents Compared with Census Education Data

	Sample		Census	
Primary School or Less	171	17.7	35,969	34.0
Some High School	278	23.8	35,733	33.8
High School Graduate	265	27.5	25,185	23.8
Some College	105	10.9	3,850	3.7
College Graduate and Post graduate	146	15.1	4,964	4.7
Total	965	100.0	105,701	100.0

Source: Derived from Dominion Bureau of Statistics, *1961 Census, Population (General Characteristics),* (Ottawa: Queen's Printer, 1962), Vol. 1–Part 3, "Schooling by Age Groups," pp. 100–106, Table 100: Population 5–24 Years of Age Attending School, by Highest Grade Attended, Five-Year Age Groups and Sex, 1961, and pp. 104–108, Table 104: Population 10 years of Age and Over Not Attending School, by Highest Grade Attended, Specific Age Groups and Sex, 1961.

Note: *N* excludes 19 respondents under 19 years of age and 16 no-response respondents.

decade earlier. For example, full-time enrollment of the University of Western Ontario, between the year 1960-1961 and 1970-1971 has grown from 4,177 to 13,987 students. This represents an increase of 335 percent over the ten-year period. If the 1961 figure 8.1 percent) is multiplied by 335 percent the resulting expected figure for 1970 is 27.1 percent compared with the 26 percent recorded.

Family Income. Table 3.5 shows that one-fifth (22.3 percent) of the people in the sample had family incomes of less than $5,000; a little over one-third (36.3 percent) of the respondents had family incomes somewhere between $5,000 and $10,000. In addition, another one-third (32.6 percent) of the sample had family incomes in excess of $10,000. Because of inflation and the significant increase in disposable family income during the last ten years, a comparison of the sample population with the 1961 Census figures would not be meaningful and therefore is not included. Finally, 9 percent of the respondents did not know their income or refused to answer this question.

However, data provided by the Dominion Bureau of Statistics based on a sample survey in 1967 indicated a median family income at that time of $7,860 and preliminary income data for 1969 show that the average family income in 1969 in Ontario rose 16 percent.[c] If the London figures increased at the rate of

---

[c]Personal correspondence from J.R. Podoluk, Co-ordinator, Consumer Finance Research Staff, Dominion Bureau of Statistics, Ottawa, July 1971.

Table 3–5
Respondents' Total Family Income From All Sources

	Number	Percentage
Not working, no income	36	3.6
Less than $3,000	95	9.5
$3,000–$4,999	92	9.2
$5,000–$6,999	126	12.6
$7,000–$9,999	237	23.7
$10,000–$14,999	215	21.5
$15,000–$19,999	54	5.4
$20,000–$24,999	29	2.9
$25,000 and Over	28	2.8
Refuse to answer, don't know	88	8.8
Total	1,000	100.0

Median Family Income = $8,350

Table 3–6
Sex to Employment Status of Respondents

	Male Percentage	Female Percentage	Combined Sample Percentage
Working	73.0	32.7	51.7
Not Working	27.0	67.3	48.3
Total	100.0	100.0	100.0
	N = 471	N = 529	N = 1,000

the provincial average, the median family income in 1969 would be approximately $9,100. However, the increase in unemployment in 1970 and our overrepresentation of students living alone would tend to depress the median family income reported by our sample.

Employment. Table 3.7 indicates that 73 percent of males and 33 percent of females were employed. The 27 percent males not working appears high unless one considers that 9.3 percent of males were students and 10.8 percent were over 65. This means that only approximately 7 percent of the sample of males who were listed as unemployed were neither students or over 65. Data from Federal Manpower Office indicated that for Ontario as a whole, the male unemployment rate in November 1970 was 4.71; data treating London only were not available. The slight overrepresentation of unemployed males is not unusual in surveys in view of the fact that the unemployed are more likely to be at home.

Table 3-7
Occupational Status Scores of Respondents

	Male Percentage	Female Percentage	Combined Sample Percentage
Lower Status (39 and below on Blishen Scale)	41.8	21.7	31.2
Middle Status (40–59 on Blishen Scale)	30.8	37.4	34.3
Upper Status (60 and above on Blishen Scale)	16.6	8.9	12.5
Student	9.3	5.5	7.3
Not Working*	0.2	23.3	12.4
No Response	1.3	3.2	2.3
Total	100.0	100.0	100.0
	N = 471	N = 529	N = 1,000

*Includes Housewives

The socio-economic status of the sample respondents was evaluated and coded using the Blishen Socio-Economic Index for occupations in Canada.[d] This scheme evaluates the occupational levels in Candada, based on the 1961 Census data, assigning approximations of the Pineo-Porter prestige scale to census occupational titles. (The scale is reproduced in the Appendix.) In order to approximate high, middle, and low status occupational levels, all occupations listed at 60 or above on the Blishen Sclae were categorized as high status occupations, 40 through 59 were categorized as middle status occupations, and 39 or less as low status occupations. For ease of presentation, respondents will be classified as having high status occupations, middle status occupations or low status occupations.

Table 3.7 indicates that approximately 31 percent of the respondents were classified as having low status occupations, one-third (34.3 percent) of them were classified as middle status, and one-eighth (12.5 percent) were high status. One-fifth (19.7 percent) of the respondents were either students, housewives, or unemployed.

In summary, significant sociodemographic characteristics (age, marital status, religion, education, family income, employment status, and social status of the sample) were described and compared with available census data. Where such comparisons were justified, the characteristics of the sample population resembled the census population to a marked degree. These sociodemographic variables will be used throughout the study wherever we wish to characterize

---

[d]Bernard Blishen, "A Socio-Economic Index for Occupations in Canada," *The Canadian Review of Sociology and Anthropology,* Vol. 4, 1967, 41-54.

communications behavior by our respondents in terms of their social characteristics.

The Off-the-Air Radio Study Methodology

The source of data for this report was a sample of radio phone-in shows aired in London, Ontario, during the summer and fall of 1970 and the winter and spring of 1971. The sample consisted of programs presented on AM radio by stations CFPL, CJOE and CKSL, that is, all the AM stations located in London.

A total of 84 programs were monitored and recorded on tape. A total of 3,226 calls were recorded. From these tapes, summaries were then made of each day's programs, call by call. Each summary included the sex of the caller, the duration in seconds of the call, a precis of the call's content as well as the host's response to the caller. Following this, each call was coded and then transferred to IBM cards, which were then put on computer tape for statistical analysis. Following is the breakdown of stations, times and samples.

CFPL. CFPL is the only radio station with this type of program which has consistently broadcast in the 6:30-10:30 *A.M.* time period, Monday through Saturday, throughout the year. All told, 50 programs were monitored in the periods July to October 1970 and February to May 1971, for a total of 196 hours and 20 minutes. Shows were taped during the last week of one month beginning on a Monday and the first week of the following month.

CJOE. This station removed its phone-in radio shows from its programing after October 1970 and therefore only 24 programs were monitored, for a total of 94 hours and 50 minutes. This corresponds to the number of shows monitored from CFPL for the same period. The program was aired daily from 6:30-10:30 *A.M.,* Monday through Saturday. The same method of selecting programs as was used for CFPL was followed.

CKSL. CKSL did not have a phone-in show in either July or August 1970. The idea was introduced in September, but was not very successful and was dropped after October 1970. The programs were monitored, between 5 *P.M.* and 6:30 *P.M.* weekdays, for a total of 14 hours and 15 minutes. The same method of selecting programs as was used for other stations was followed.

The Information Center: Methodology

The objectives of the present research are to study the pattern of usage of a typical information center in order to discern the kinds of needs expressed, the channels used to express them and the relationship of the two factors to the sociological characteristics of clients.

The three basic kinds of data to be analyzed, then, consist of:

1. A brief sociological description of users.
2. The categories of their inquiries.
3. The means used to inquire (i.e., telephone, interview).

The Background of Information London

Information London is a community-based information center, which began operation in November 1970 with the aid of small grants received from provincial, municipal, and federal agencies. Its terms of reference were that it was to function as "an information and referral center to help the general public make more effective use of available community services, facilities, and resources, both public and voluntary . . . "[e]

The terms of reference spelled out in the original proposal suggested a two-fold purpose.

1. The collection of information, i.e., functioning as an "information bank" to include information concerning federal, provincial, municipal and community resources available to individuals.
2. Referral of individuals to "appropriate sources for further assistance."[f]

In 1971, Information London summarized its first six months of operation (November 30, 1970 through May 31, 1971) and presented the following information.

1. A total of 2,855 inquiries were processed.
2. Females were clients in 66 percent of inquiries and males represented 34 percent of such inquiries.
3. Of 25 percent of callers who could be identified, Information London workers believed 150 were "young people," 112 were "elderly" and 152 were "newcomers or immigrants."
4. There were wide variations in the kinds of inquiries made, "from inquiries about the correct spelling of a word or the location of a street, to grave emotional, social or family problems. Inquiries dealt with almost every facet of daily living: accommodation, child care, landlord-tenant relations, legal assistance, and recreation to name a few."[g]
5. In February, 92 callers were asked a series of questions of whom 61 agreed to

---

[e]Letter proposal to the Department of the Secretary of State, Ottawa, from Information London, July 1970.
[f]Ibid.
[g]John Kennedy and Lynda MacGilliuary, Information London, Six Month Report, 1971.

answer. Sex, age, marital status, education, employment status, occupation, income level and time of residence were questions asked. Because of the time required, mostly on the telephone, and sensitivity of the questions, there was an unacceptably large refusal rate; this combined with the smallness of the sample suggests the results are of limited validity.

This early pilot study revealed to the present investigator the necessity of reducing the number of questions to be asked of the client to the barest minimum that would provide useful data which would help to identify the sociological characteristics of the caller. The questions, then, ideally should be capable of being asked in approximately five seconds following the inquirer's request. Since in virtually all cases gender was discernible, age and education were selected as questions to be asked.

The data of the information center research was collected in July, August, and September of 1971 by Information London workers. The method was telephone interview of clients who were calling Information London for information, advice or help. In addition, some clients were "walk in"types and were personally interviewed.

During normal operations, the information center worker fills out a standardized form which indicates the category of information or aid requested and the disposition of the request. This form is also used by a great number of other information centers, facilitating the gathering of substantial amounts of statistical information (see Appendix). The relevant information includes the way in which contact was made — (telephone, interview, corespondence); who inquired (individual, another person in behalf of an individual or a governmental or welfare agency), the type of inquiry (routine requests for names, addresses or deeper knowledge of community resources, policies, etc.), an attempt to identify special groupings of inquirers (aged, youth, handicapped, etc.), and category of inquiry and disposition.

It should be noted that as in all coding schemes which attempt to categorize human communication and behavior, the fit of such a form to the many variations in needs and they way in which they are expressed, along with the subjective interpretations of the coder (in this case, the information center worker) makes possible much room for error. These data forms are constantly being assessed in terms of their fit to the changing needs of the population.

During the months of July, August, and September, a total of 1,911 forms were filled out containing the category of information requested. Of these, sex of the respondent was available for 1,886 cases, age was provided for 1,341, and education was provided for 1,187. It should be noted that cases for which such information was not provided represented the following reasons.

1. Error of the interviewer who may have forgotten to ask.
2. Heavy workload and ensuing time problem (e.g., while handling one client, others are calling on alternative lines).

3. Unknown, because request came from third party.

4. Refusals by clients.

Where a third party requested help on behalf of another he or she was asked for the information if they could be certain it was accurate.

The table analyses upon which this report was based represent total cases (where descriptive tables are presented) and on the total sample of respondents for which information was available where cross-tabulation analysis is employed, i.e., the sample size where education is a variable will be 1,187 rather than 1,911.

Upon completion of interviewing, forms were transposed to IBM cards and then to tape, where they were utilized in computer analysis of the data.

4 Letters to the Editor

The daily newspaper is the oldest and largest mass communication institution in London, Ontario, and when we speak of the daily newspaper, the *London Free Press*, we observe that of the 89 percent of the sample population who take a daily newspaper, nearly all (97 percent) receive the *London Free Press*. Another 10 percent of newspaper buyers receive the *Toronto Globe and Mail*.

The pattern of use of the letters column must be considered in the context of the earlier mentioned unpublished study on rates, which indicates that smaller towns with parochial newspapers generally generate a lower per-hundred-papers-sold rate of letters sent than the high quality quasi-national newspaper, such as the *Globe and Mail*. Conversely, the probability of a letter being published, once it has been sent, is higher for smaller newspapers.

Approximately 1.8 letters are sent per 100 copies of the *London Free Press* sold and the probability that a letter will be published is 80 percent. The probability that a letter will be sent depends on the socioeconomic profile of the readership of a newspaper. In the present study, the median family income of subscribers to the *Globe and Mail* only was $15,000 and for the *London Free Press* $8,500. Approximately 3.5 letters are sent per 100 copies of the *Toronto Globe and Mail* sold and the probability that a letter will be published is 36 percent. A related factor with respect to readership is education. The typical *Globe and Mail* reader had completed two or more years of university while the typical *Free Press* reader had achieved a grade twelve level.

Another aspect – the kinds of interests of the readers – may influence whether an individual will be stimulated to write. Seventy percent of *Globe and Mail* subscribers stated they purchased it because of its national and international coverage while only 14 percent of the *Free Press* subscribers gave this as the reason.

How Many People Write

The survey did not ask to which newspaper the individual wrote, but merely whether he had ever written a letter to a newspaper. The results indicated that an overwhelming percentage of the respondents had never written a letter to a newspaper. Only 9 percent of the sample had ever written a letter to a newspaper (table 4.1). Across Canada, English language daily newspapers receive

Table 4–1

**Have You Ever Written a Letter to the Letters-to-the Editor Column
in a Newspaper?**

	Number	Percentage
No	904	90.4
Yes	91	9.1
No Response	5	0.5
Total	1,000	100.0

3.0 letters per 100 papers sold, according to data for 1970 (Singer and Cameron, 1971).

Approximately 5 percent of the sample had written a letter to the editor during the past two years. Single letter writers amounted to 3.7 percent and those who wrote two, three, four or more amounted to one-half percent each of the sample (table 4.2). Approximately 73 percent of all individuals who wrote letters sent one and 27 percent of this subsample sent more than one (table 4.2). Thus, it appears that even of the small percentage of individuals who have ever written letters, few are "regulars."

Description of the Sample

Sex of Letter Writers. Males are more likely than females to write letters to newspapers. Approximately 58 percent of the letter writers were male and 42 percent were female (table 4.3).

Age of Letter Writers. The letter writer could not be distinguished from the non-letter writer in terms of median age. The median for both categories was 38 years (table 4.4). The evidence seems to contradict past research that letter writers tend to be elderly on one hand, or else there is a trend toward more letter writing by individuals in the lower age ranges than was once so. Comparison of table 4.4 distribution with table 3.1 (distribution of the sample in Chapter 3) does not indicate any significant overrepresentation by any age category.

Education of Letter Writers. The median educational level of those who had written a letter was grade 13, compared with grade 12 for those who had not written a letter. A comparison of letter writers with the sample distribution of table 4.5 indicates differences, however.

The comparison of distributions leaves no doubt that lower educational categories are highly underrepresented and higher educational categories are

Table 4-2
How Many Letters Have You Written in the Past Two Years? How Many Were Published?

Number of Letter Writers	Number of Letters Written	Number of Letters Sent	Percentage of All Letters Sent	Number of Letters Published	Percentage of Letters Published to Letters Sent
37	1	37	44.0	27	73.0
5	2	10	11.9	8	80.0
5	3	15	17.9	5	33.3
4	4 or more	22	26.2	2	9.1
Total 51		84	100.0	42	

Note: N excludes "No Response" and "Unknown" cases.

Table 4–3

Sex of Respondents. Have you Ever Written a Letter to the Editor?

	Yes		No		No Response		Total	
Male	54	11.4	413	87.8	4	0.8	471	100.0
Female	37	7.0	491	92.8	1	0.2	529	100.0
Total	91	9.1	904	90.4	5	0.5	1,000	100.0

Note: N excludes "No Response" and "Unknown" cases.

Table 4–4

Age Distribution of Letter Writers Compared with Sample

	Letter Writers	Sample
Up to 19	1.1	1.9
20–24	21.6	17.7
25–29	13.6	14.2
30–34	5.7	9.1
35–39	12.5	10.4
40–44	10.2	8.0
45–49	6.8	9.1
50–54	8.0	7.1
55–59	6.8	7.0
60–64	2.3	3.5
65–69	1.1	3.8
70–74	6.8	3.5
75–79	1.1	3.0
80 and Over	2.3	1.7
Total	99.9	99.9

Note: N excludes 3 "No Response" cases.

Table 4–5

Educational Distribution of Letter Writers Compared with Sample

	Letter Writers	Sample
Primary School	10.1	17.4
Some High School	14.6	28.5
High School Graduate	29.2	28.8
Some College	22.5	10.7
College Graduate and Postgraduate	23.6	14.5
Total	100.0	99.9
	$N = 89$	$N = 950$

Note: No Response-Unknown answers excluded from base.

Table 4-6
Income Distribution of Letter Writers Compared With Sample

Family Income	Letter Writers	Sample
Below $5,000	30.4	24.4
$5,000–$9,999	23.6	39.8
$10,000–$14,999	24.7	23.6
$15,000–$19,999	12.4	5.9
$20,000 and Above	7.8	6.3
Total	99.9	100.0

Note: "No Response" answers excluded from base.

highly overrepresented. Letters to the editor columns undoubtedly can be characterized as the domain of the well educated in our society.

Income of Letter Writers. Although the median family income of those who had written letters to the editor is higher than that of those who had not ($9,400 to $8,200), comparison of the distributions of letter writers with the sample reveals interesting differences (see table 4.6).

It is clear that those in the very low income categories (below $5,000) and those in the high income categories ($15,000 and over) are overrepresented among letter writers. The low to middle categories ($5,000 to $9,999) are substantially underrepresented. One meaning to be derived from this pattern is that those who are the most deprived in terms of financial rewards and those who are in the highest financial reward categories use this forum to gain their objectives while those in the middle do not find themselves particularly aroused and less often feel compelled to express themselves through this channel. This is in contradistinction to the previous findings of the high education level of letter writers; there is a substantial sociological literature that treats the problem of "status inconsistency" (one example is high education with financial rewards that are below expected for a particular educational attainment) (Elton Jackson, 1962). Future studies of letter writing as well as other kinds of participation may well address this problem.

Success in Getting Letter Published

Earlier, it was indicated that 9 percent of the sample had ever written a letter to a newspaper. To write a letter does not assure, of course, that it will be published, in view of the fact that editors, functioning as gatekeepers, may screen out the inarticulate, as well as the libelous, the controversial and the uneducated.

In fact, only 6 percent of the sample or approximately two-thirds of those who had sent letters had ever had a letter published (table 4.7). Although cells are small, some data are available on the socioeconomic correlates of success in getting one's letter published. The median age of the successful was higher than that of the unsuccessful (41 years of age compared with 34 years). By collapsing the age categories, we should be able to establish which age categories are most and least successful. The age comparisons indicate a positive pattern of relationships between age and success in getting a letter published.

Sex is also related to the probability of publication. Seventy-two percent of letters sent by males were published compared with 57 percent of letters sent by females.

No pattern of differences emerges with respect to education, with the successful and unsuccessful letter writers both having a median education of 12 years. The distribution showed no discernible differences either.

There is a relationship between family income and the probability of having a letter published. The median income of successful writers was $9,360 and that of unsuccessful writers, $8,840. Approximately 62 percent of individuals who wrote with incomes below $10,000 had letters published and approximately 74 percent of those with incomes above $10,000 were successful.

Another factor that seems to be related to whether a letter will be published is the issue of the number of letters written. During the past two years, 73 percent of those who sent one letter saw them in print and 80 percent of those who sent two letters were successful. But of those who wrote three, only 33 percent were published and of those who wrote four, only 9 percent were published (i.e., four individuals were responsible for 22 letters sent during the past two years, but reported only two were published) (table 4.2) Thus, the prolific letter writer is a notable failure in terms of percentages. It may be that the prolific letter writer is one who is easily and often aroused and doesn't choose his words well; our data, however, offer no concrete evidence that such is the explanation.

What They Write About

Individuals write about a wide variety of topics, from personal complaints about service at a local establishment to statements about treatment of animals to comments expressing their attitudes on politics, social issues, and institutions. The content — that is, the universe of their discourse — will be found to vary somewhat from that found in other feedback media. Opinions on politics, social issues and local problems represent the majority of letter topics. Table 4.8 provides a breakdown of the topic areas.

Another way of viewing the letters written is in terms of form rather than content. When the answers were recoded in terms of the question, "what was the manifest purpose rather than substantive content?", 54 of the answers could be categorized as indicated in table 4.9.

Table 4-7
Success in Letter Publishing and Age

Age	Success in Having Letter Published (percentage)
Up to 24	60.0
25–39	64.3
40–59	66.7
60 and Over	72.7

Table 4-8
Topics of Letter Writers

Topic*	Number	Percentage
1. Politics, government and social issues of the day	18	27.7
2. Local issues & services	11	16.9
3. Education	9	13.8
4. Sports & Special Events	9	13.8
5. Mass Media	7	10.7
6. Animals	3	4.6
7. Complaints of a personal nature or dealing with products or services	3	4.6
8. Health & Housing	3	4.6
9. Other & Miscellaneous	2	3.1
Total	65	100.0

Note: A total of 65 individuals answered this question in such a way that the categories could be coded.

*See Appendix for coding breakdown.

Table 4-9
Purpose of Letters

Purpose of Letter	Number	Percentage
To give information	2	3.7
To get information	2	3.7
To give opinion on topic	18	33.3
To give an opinion on a local issue	13	24.1
To give an opinion on a national issue	2	3.7
To give an opinion on an international issue	0	0.0
To praise	2	3.7
Media complaints	7	13.0
General complaints	8	14.8
Total	54	100.0

Note: N excludes "No Response" and "Unknown" cases.

Examination of the two preceding tables indicates that the letters column provides an opportunity for opinion presentation, which is the leading category; that local issues prevail when compared with general topics and with national and international issues; and that the information and ombudsman functions are quite minor.

In the next chapter we shall examine the ombudsman function of the newspaper.

References

Jackson, Elton F. "Status Consistency and Symptoms of Stress." *American Sociological Review* 27, 4 (August 1962): 469-80.

Singer, Benjamin D. and Cameron, Andrew D. *Letters to the Editor.* An unpublished study, 1971.

5 The Urban Newspaper Ombudsman

While governmental ombudsmen concern themselves with complaints concerning government departments, the newspaper ombudsman tends to deal with a wider range of problems; and rather than having official status, his effectiveness is "related to the social control powers of the newspaper itself. . . . By naming the offending merchant, company, or agency in the published sample cases, the action columnist is clearly making use of this power of social control" (Hannigan, 1972: 38-39). In addition, as Hannigan has also pointed out, the newspaper ombudsman has, through his extensive experience, developed great knowledge of effective channels.

The procedures employed by the *London Free Press* ombudsman, Gordon Sanderson, are rather straightforward. A client is required to write except in rare cases. It is assumed the complainant has attempted to settle his problem with the source of the complaint and has failed. The column receives close to 5,000 letters per year and approximately 15 percent are published in the paper (Hannigan, 1972: 41-43).

However, the use of this channel is relatively rare compared to other channels studied in this book. Only 4 percent of the sample had ever contacted the column, which had been started in 1967 and has been under the stewardship of Gordon Sanderson since then. The popularity of the column has been such that its once three-times-a-week appearance has been increased to daily.

It is because of the small size of this subsample (4 percent) that few detailed cross-tabulations could be employed.

Description of the Sample

Sex of the User. Males more often complained to "Sound Off." Approximately 4-1/2 percent of males compared with 3.6 percent of the females had called upon the column for help.

Age of the User. The median user was 36 years of age and the median age of the non-user was 38 years, approximately the same as letter writers. Cells were too small to compare the frequency distribution with the sample.

Education of Users. The median education level of the column's users was 11 and that of non-users was 12. The distribution when compared to the sample

41

Table 5-1

Education Distribution of "Sound Off" Users Compared With Sample

Education Level	Users	Sample
Primary School	18.0	17.5
Some High School	38.5	28.4
High School Graduate	28.2	28.9
Some College	7.7	10.6
College Graduate and Postgraduate	7.7	14.5
Total	100.1	99.9

indicates the column is most typically used by individuals low in formal education (table 5.1).

It is not the very bottom level, but those with some formal education, but not a lot, who on one hand may get themselves more involved with firms and agencies that they can't handle. On the other hand, respondents in the very lowest educational category may get just as involved, but may not be as aware of the help such a column can provide or be too apathetic to use it.

Income of Users. There was little difference in the income levels of the user and non-user. The income of the former was $8,350 and that of the non-user was $8,200. Because cells were too small, comparison of frequencies would not be fruitful. However, one cell – the $7,000 to $9,999 category – was overrepresented, inasmuch as 36 percent of all users fell there compared with 24 percent of the sample. This may simply reflect the fact that with higher income, such individuals make more financial commitments, of which a certain percentage will inevitably involve some problem with the company. The median income of the user is higher than the non-user, thus it is possible they are the ones who have the income to involve themselves but not the sophistication that comes with education to handle the problem themselves.

Reasons for Contacting Sound Off

A total of 38 individuals provided reasons why they contacted "Sound Off." Of these, nearly two-thirds concerned consumer problems (63 percent), 18 percent concerned problems with the government, and less than 3 percent each were concerned with media, health, education and welfare, and employment problems, as is indicated in table 5.2.

Hannigan's study on a different population (rather than a general population, he used a sample drawn from those who had contacted "Sound Off") revealed that the highest ranking consumer problem was failure to receive merchandise,

Table 5-2
Over What Issue Did You Contact "Sound Off"?

	Number	Percentage
Consumer Problems*	24	63.2
Government Problems	7	18.4
Other	4	10.5
Media Problems	1	2.6
Health, Education, and Welfare Problems	1	2.6
Employment Problems	1	2.6
Animal Problems	0	0.0
Discrimination Problems	0	0.0
Culture and Special Events	0	0.0
Sports and Hobby	0	0.0
Total	38	99.9

Note: *N* excludes "No Response" cases.

*For an explanation of the coding categories employed here, see Appendix.

followed by defective merchandise or repair work and then lack of refund for goods (Hannigan, 1972: 75).

One factor that distinguishes the newspaper ombudsman from other media feedback institutions is that results are more often direct and measurable. This is because the communication from the aggrieved individual is usually specific and calls for specific action for an individual rather than referring to a class of individuals as is more often the case where individuals write letters expressing their opinions to the newspaper letters column.

The more intensive study of the sample of column users themselves by Hannigan also revealed that 91 percent of the column's clients had attempted to clear up their grievance with the subject of it prior to contacting "Sound Off" and that nearly a third had simply been ignored. Approximately 20 percent had been promised action, but received none and approximately one-sixth had had their complaint denied because of alleged lack of responsibility or liability by the subject of the complaint (Hannigan, 1972: 79). A limited amount of information was available concerning results, in response to the question, "What action resulted from contacting Sound Off?" Approximately 55 percent reported positive action, 33 percent reported no action, 3 percent (one person) indicated action was still in progress and approximately 5 percent (two persons) indicated their situation became worse. The fact that one-third of the respondents reported no action is possibly explained in great part by cases in which the complaint was not justified to one extent or another, in addition to those cases involving lack of cooperation by the firm or agency which was the subject of the complaint.

In general, users of the column feel it is a fairly effective way of achieving results, for 73 percent of Hannigan's sample said they would again contact the column in the event of similar problems in the future (Hannigan, 1972: 94).

References

Hannigan, John A. "The Newspaper Ombudsman and the Redress of Consumer Complaints." Master's thesis, University of Western Ontario, 1972.

6 The Radio Call-In Show

The Survey

The radio call-in show has become a North American institution during the 1960s. In London, CFPL began broadcasting its "Open Line" show in 1961 and this name quickly became virtually a synonym for such shows in the London area. The two other local AM stations added such programs in 1968 (CKSL) and 1970 (CJOE). However, theirs have been on-again-off-again situations while the CFPL program has been on uninterruptedly for the past decade. The call-in shows are popular or liked by approximately 60 percent of the sample and disliked by 40 percent. Prior to examining the data concerning usage, it would be of interest to know why individuals like or dislike such programs.

As can be seen in table 6.1, the highest response category was "Information" followed by "Contact with people," liking for the show's host, a chance to express one's opinion, that it is controversial and finally that it solves problems.

On the other hand, as is indicated in table 6.2, most objections to call-in shows were based on the "mentality of callers," followed by dislike of the host, the airing of prejudices, blandness, too many such shows, and finally the controversial nature of the shows.

Table 6-1
What Do You Like About Open-Line Programs

	Number	Percentage
Information	161	28.8
Contact with people	121	22.7
Likes commentator	78	14.0
Chance to express opinion	68	12.2
Don't Know	64	11.5
Controversial	43	7.7
Problem solving	23	4.1
Total	558	100.0

Note: N excludes 385 respondents who disliked open-line programs and 57 respondents who did not indicate whether they liked or disliked open-line programs.

Table 6–2
What Do You Dislike About Open-Line Programs?

	Number	Percentage
Low mentality of callers	151	39.2
Dislike commentator	73	19.0
Don't Know	67	17.4
Airing of Prejudices	40	10.4
Too Middle of the Road	27	7.0
Too many open-line shows	16	4.2
Too controversial	11	2.9
Total	385	100.1

Note: *N* excludes 558 respondents who liked open-line programs and 57 respondents who did not indicate whether they liked or disliked open-line programs.

How Many People Use the Call-In Show?

It was surprising to find how much more widespread the use of the call-in show is than is true for printed counterparts. Approximately 20 percent of the sample had called such a show in the past. Table 6.3 indicates the frequency of usage.

The radio call-in show, when compared with letters to the editor, does appear to indicate greater use by "regulars," i.e., individuals who have used it more than once, although the data are not, strictly speaking, comparable (the latter asked number of letters sent during the past two years and indicated 73 percent had sent only one). It is also possible that individuals underestimated the number of times they had phoned because of the cultural stricture concerning telephone use (i.e., being a "telephone gabber").

Description of the Sample

Sex of the Caller. It was not surprising to find that 63 percent of those who said they had called such a show were female, compared with 37 percent male (the comparable sample statistics were 53 percent female and 47 percent male), for the shows have been predominantly morning shows when the male of the household is more likely to be at work.

Age of the Caller. The median age of the callers was 40 years and of the non-callers 36 years. An examination of table 6.4 indicates that callers in age categories under 35 are underrepresented, the cumulative frequency of callers being 37 percent compared with 43 percent for the sample. The callers in age categories 35-59 are overrepresented 50 percent to 42 percent in the sample. For

Table 6–3
Frequency of Usage of Phone-In Shows

	Number	Percentage of All Users
Once	120	62
Few Times	71	36
Quite Often	4	2
Total	195	100

Note: *N* excludes "No Response" cases.

Table 6–4
Age Distributions of Callers and Sample

Age	Callers	Sample
Up to 19	2.1	2.0
20–24	14.3	17.7
25–29	13.2	14.2
30–34	7.4	9.1
35–39	12.2	10.4
40–44	8.5	8.0
45–49	10.1	9.1
50–54	11.1	7.1
55–59	7.9	7.0
60–64	3.7	3.5
65–69	3.2	3.8
70–74	3.7	3.5
75–79	2.1	3.0
80 and Over	0.5	1.7
Total	100.0	100.1

Note: *N* excludes "No Response" cases.

callers 60 and over, there are approximately 13 percent compared with approximately 16 percent in the sample.

Education of Callers. The median education for callers and non-callers was 12 years. Table 6.5 indicates the distributions.

Although the median education is the same, the distribution comparison reveals that the very low, the high, and the very high education groups are underrepresented among callers, while the low education and middle group (some high school, and high school graduates) are overrepresented among callers. The radio call-in show appears to be a phenomenon dominated by the lower middle and middle education groups.

Income of Callers. The median income of callers was $8,800 and that of non-callers was $8,200. When the distributions are compared, there is slight underrepresentation among callers in the lower income groupings and slight overrepresentation in categories of $7,000 and over (see table 6.6). Actually, the income distribution of radio show callers corresponds more closely to the sample than is true for either letters to the editor or the use of the "Sound Off" column.

Topics of Calls, Purposes of Calls

We are making the same distinction here as was made for letters to newspapers, having coded separately for topics and for purpose of call. Table 6.7 presents the eight topic areas indicated by the sample.

As can be seen, the leading topics, in order, were politics, government and social issues of the day, animals, and sports and special events, which together constituted more than half the respondents' answers.

Table 6.8 indicates the distribution of answers coded for the purpose of the call. The table indicates that the largest number of calls related to the giving or getting of information, approximately 38 percent, followed by the opinion presentation categories, approximately 24 percent. Such radio programs, therefore, serve more importantly as an information source than for opinion presentation.

The Off the Air Study

The sample survey was able to provide a range of interesting data on the appeal of such shows, on the users of such shows, their social characteristics and the way in which use is made. However, there are other facts which would amplify the picture provided, but which cannot be gleaned from interviews with any degree of accuracy. For example, one way of examining the proposition that such programs are essentially expressive, cathartic for many people, the so-called "blowing off steam" function suggested by some writers as explanations for media feedback, might be to take a somewhat phenomenalistic perspective, to examine the details of the call itself, the duration of the call, its proximate stimulus, etc.

And, in addition, it would be of interest to know whether there is a time or season relationship with the calls from which we might infer something of the impulse basis versus that of a perhaps intense underlying problem. Thus, if during poor weather, calls increase, one inference may be that situational factors – sheer listenership and access to a telephone – may account for a significant proportion of the higher usage recorded.

Table 6-5

Education Distributions of Callers and Sample

Education	Callers	Sample
Primary School or less	13.6	17.5
Some High School	35.1	28.5
High School Graduate	34.6	28.8
Some College	6.8	10.7
College Graduate & Postgraduate	9.9	14.5
Total	100.0	100.0

Note: *N* excludes "No Response" Cases.

Table 6-6

Income of Callers and Sample

	Callers	Sample
No Income	2.2	4.0
Up to $3,000	8.9	10.4
$3,000–$4,999	12.8	10.1
$5,000–$6,999	9.5	13.8
$7,000–$9,999	27.4	25.9
$10,000–$14,999	25.1	23.6
$15,000–$19,999	7.3	5.9
$20,000–$24,999	3.9	3.2
$25,000 and Over	2.8	3.1
Total	99.9	100.0

Table 6-7

Topics of Open Line Callers

Topic	Number	Per Cent
1. Politics, government and social issues of the day	38	23.8
2. Local issues and services	22	13.8
3. Education	8	5.0
4. Sports and special events	23	14.4
5. The Mass Media	10	6.2
6. Animals	26	16.2
7. Complaints of a personal nature or dealing with products or services	20	12.5
8. Health and Housing	11	6.9
9. Other and Miscellaneous	2	1.2
Total	160	100.0

Note: A total of 160 individuals provided answers that could be coded.
N excludes "No Response" cases.

Table 6–8

Purpose of Calls to Open Line

Purpose of Call	Percentage
Give information	17.0
Get information	20.9
Give opinion on Topic	12.4
Give opinion on local issue	8.5
Give opinion on national issue	1.7
Give opinion on international issue	1.1
To praise	2.8
Media complaints	1.7
General Complaints	9.6
Lost & Found	9.6
Straw vote	3.4
Get help	4.5
Offer help	.6
Joke	.6
Offer items	3.4
Mediator corrections	2.3
Total	100.1

Note: N excludes "No Response" cases.

Finally, we might want to know more about process factors per se: what happens to the call with respect to the host's response? This question helps us to cast further light on the reason for the use of this channel.

The present study works with a different kind of sample than the survey to attempt to assess the process of such phone calls in greater depth. It utilizes the actual calls, as taped from the air, rather than what individuals tell us about their past calls. The advantages of the present technique balance the disadvantages. The advantages include accuracy, extensiveness (the total message is analyzed rather than a statement about it), the ability to measure the time of the message, the day of week, month, and season, and the host's response.

The data, derived from a total of 84 programs of this nature, were recorded on tape, comprising 3,226 calls, and include the voice of the caller, the content of the call, and the response of the host.

Time and Duration

There was a consistent pattern of calls throughout each week; however the number did vary substantially by season. Spring and winter produced the largest number of calls per program, 56 and 55 respectively, with fall accounting for 44 and summer, 33. Since this somewhat follows the pattern of listening as it would be affected by weather (and, undoubtedly, ready access to a phone), it also lends support to the notion that a substantial number of the calls *may* be of a

Table 6–9
Duration of Calls

	Number	Per Cent
0–30 seconds	706	21.2
31–59 seconds	1,058	33.2
1–1.59 minutes	922	29.0
2–3 minutes	293	9.2
Greater than 3 minutes	202	6.4
Total	3,181	100.0

Note: *N* excludes 45 indeterminate cases.

relatively impulsive nature, in fact may be stimulated by the medium itself, that hearing other calls or the host's opinion is a major stimulus for calling. This will be explored later as well.

Call duration varied from less than 20 seconds to greater than three minutes (table 6.9), with 31-59 seconds being the most typical length, followed by 1-1.59 minutes and then 30 seconds or less. More than half of all calls (55 percent) were less than a minute in length. This aspect is in great part controlled by the host, but also is a function of the kind of call, e.g., announcements of events, simple requests for information or answers would tend to affect these figures, perhaps lowering them. But these data tend to argue against the notion that such programs provide long, drawn-out cathartic sessions or are primarily elongated gossip sessions. However, they also argue against another image, that of the quasi-resurrection of early town hall meetings, for, since time constraints most often result in a truncated statement from the caller rather than a leisurely exchange of opinion, they can by no means constitute a modern-day reappearance of the fully participational town hall.

The Proximate Stimulus

There are a number of explanations for the use of channels such as this. Individuals with longstanding and pervasive complaints may call, as may others with concerns generated in the immediate past. The seasonal variation described earlier suggested the hypothesis that many of the calls may well have had a proximate stimulus located in the fact of the medium itself, that hearing other calls or the host's opinion may have stimulated the call. The content analysis was able to establish two broadly different categories of calls: those which were manifestly independent of previous calls or statements on the program or of other media and those which manifestly had references or correlates. These are shown in table 6.10.

Table 6-10
Call Stimuli

	Number	Percentage
Independent	1,593	49.38
Response to previous calls on same subject	1,319	40.89
Response to issues raised by other media	159	4.93
Response to Host's remarks, questions, etc.	114	3.53
Response to a commentary	39	1.21
No response	2	0.06
Total	3,226	100.00

As is indicated by table 6.10 the largest category of calls was, in fact, independent of other material carried on the program; however, as is indicated in another part of this book, these programs nevertheless carry a higher percentage of contacts which are a result of stimuli carried by the medium itself than is true of letters to the editor.

We can throw more light on the proximate stimulus-to-response phenomenon by examining the character of the call cross-tabulated by the proximate stimulus (see table 6.11). Coding was established on the basis of negative opinion, positive opinion, information requested, information given, and a residual category.

It can be seen that the *"independent"* category most often is associated with requests for information or aid (39 percent) followed by a *negative opinion* on a subject (24 percent). The lowest category is that of positive opinion (4 percent). The category *previous calls* is most often associated with the supplying of information or the offer of aid (40 percent), followed by negative opinion (29 percent). The lowest category is that of requesting information or aid (5 percent). The category *host* is most often associated with negative opinion (30 percent), followed by positive opinion (23 percent). The lowest category is that of requesting information or aid. The category *station commentary* is most often associated with a negative opinion call, followed by positive opinion. Finally, the category *other media* also is most often associated with a negative opinion call.

The pattern of relationships thus revealed seems very clear. Negative opinion calls are most often preceded by some content by a member of a news source: the station commentator, another medium, the host. These then appear to elicit the most so-called "agin" behavior in the words of Foster and Friedrich (cited in Grey and Brown, 1970). The latter research also indicated that most letters to newspapers were simply responses to something the individuals had already encountered in the media. Half of the calls (49 percent) in this research could not be related to any past media stimuli and, in fact, the most substantial number of calls (606) were in the category *independent information* or

Table 6-11
Proximate Stimulus and Type of Call (in Percentages)

	Indep.	Prev. Call	Host	Stat. Comm.	Other Media
Negative Opinion	24	29	30	56	47
Positive Opinion	4	21	23	21	13
Request Information, aid	39	5	8	5	16
Supply Information, aid	15	40	25	15	19
Other	24	6	16	3	5
N =	1,593	1,317	114	39	159

help-seeking. These calls were not the product of any proximate stimuli, but apparently resulted from the sheer fact that the program existed.

While it is clear that personalities within the media do stimulate a great deal of responses and it may also be true that this kind of behavior is psychologically beneficial (i.e., cathartic), the high visibility of this kind of interaction between host and caller should not be allowed to obscure the fact that the most substantial category of calls — 1,538 or 48 percent — were calls that dealt with the need or provision of information or aid.

The Host as Oracle

The continuing popularity of such programs depends upon a number of factors, and among them, if not the most important, is the relationship between the host and his audience. In part, this is a function, in turn, of the kinds of responses the host provides to callers. An attempt has been made here to describe the types of responses given by the host to callers, as shown in table 6.12.

Most often, as can be seen, the host provides a neutral response, such as, "I see," "And that is your opinion," etc. Next most often he provides a positive reinforcement, such as "That is a very good point," or "I agree with you completely." Following in order, he will pass on the question or comment to the listening audience, "Well, let's see if anybody in the audience can answer that." In some cases he answers the question directly, e.g., "The deadline for purchase of new license plates is February 28." Following in order, he provides a negative response, such as, "I think that is a preposterous statement," or "I couldn't disagree more." The last category is referral, where the host says. e.g., "For

Table 6–12
Host's Responses to Callers (in Percentages)

	Number	Percentage
Neutral	1,293	40.39
Positive response	702	21.65
Passes question	520	16.24
Answers question	437	13.64
Negative response	143	4.46
Refers or directs caller to answer	106	3.31
$N =$	3,201	

information on those kinds of benefits, I suggest you call the manpower office here in London."

The host's response, of course, is not generated in a vacuum and depends upon the character of the call. No attempt has been made to characterize calls in terms of tone, but rather the earlier categories (negative opinion, positive opinion, information-aid seeking, information-aid provision) have been cross-tabulated with the behavior of the host in order to search out any relationships between them. Table 6.13 presents the results.

As is shown in table 6.13, the host is more often positive (35 percent of the time) in response to a positive call than to a negative call (22 percent). He also provides a negative response in kind more than three times as often. Interestingly enough, the host most frequently attempts to answer questions and requests for help himself (41 percent of the time) and passes the call to the audience almost as often (39 percent of the time), followed by a referral to an outside source (8 percent of the time). Those who call in to provide information or help are responded to neutrally (59 percent of the time) or positively (23 percent of the time), followed by passing their offer on to the audience (9 percent of the time). The host is most typically neutral in his response; and most often passes the call on to the audience in the cases of requests for information or help. It comes as no surprise that the host reacts in accordance with the kinds of calls he receives.

Although it was pointed out above that the most frequent response to calls was one of neutrality, nevertheless it should also be noted that when calls requesting information or help are received, nearly nine times out of ten (89 percent of the time) the host took rather definite action, either asking the listening audience to supply the information or advice, answering the question directly, or referring the caller to another specific source. Clearly, phone show hosts are men of action; this is undoubtedly one of their strongest appeals to their clients.

Having examined the phenomenological aspects of the radio call-in show as well as the sociological factors connected with its use, there ought to be a

Table 6-13
Host's Responses to Different Kinds of Calls

	Neutral	Positive	Passes Question on to Audience	Answers	Response	Refers or Directs to Audience	Total
Negative Opinion	45.20	21.90	9.0	8.0	11.4	4.5	100.0
Positive Opinion	58.00	34.90	.8	2.8	3.5	0	100.0
Requests Information, help	6.18	4.78	38.88	41.26	.7	8.16	99.9
Gives Information, offers help	58.87	23.38	8.56	6.24	2.08	.85	98.9

further word on the importance of this new institution in our society. This can in part be gleaned from the fact that the leading phone-in show in London *airs* nearly 15,000 telephone calls annually and receives considerably more. Thus, one station broadcasts approximately seven times as many messages as London's daily newspaper prints in its letters column.

The radio phone-in show has clearly become the dominant method by which the population uses mass media for "feedback" in our society.

7

Some Psychological and other Explanations for Participation

Anomie and Communications Participation

Social critics have pointed out that one of the more serious consequences of existence in mass societies is the loss of ability to truly be able to communicate with others. This occurs as the proportion of channels which are one way compared with two-way channels increases. The concepts "alienation" and/or "anomie" are often used to characterize inhabitants of societies of this kind.

The concept "anomie" has had a long tradition in sociology, since Durkheim popularized the term to explain the psychological condition which intervened between certain states of social organization and the deviant behavior which resulted. It is closely identified with alienation. Some investigators who use it believe they are measuring a "pervasive sense of social malintegration" (Robinson and Shaver, 1969: 172). Some would argue (with Durkheim) that it reflects a state of "normlessness" in which the usual norms of society no longer are binding upon the individual. Others who opt for a definition more relevant to political life think of it as the resultant of lack of political power, the sense that the individual has no control over his individual destiny within an unresponsive social order. Powerlessness, despondency over social life, pessimism — the inability to plan or predict in a social order that is essentially unpredictable — these are both implicit and explicit in the questions of the Srole scale, which attempts to tap the presence of the anomie phenomenon.

The scale developed by Leo Srole was included in the present research in order to assess the possibility that one's access to and utilization of participatory media — the feedback systems we have been discussing — will be inversely related to the amount of anomie demonstrated. Clearly, if one does feel "cut off," incommunicado with the balance of society, then the result ought to be a high degree of anomie. And it seems clear that those authorities who believe that new communications technology will make possible greater opportunities for participation also believe that man's psychological well-being will be improved as a result of his access to and usage of these new means of expressing himself.

The hypothesis being tested is limited, however, to the following statement: the amount of anomie displayed will be inversely related to the individual's utilization of participatory media (as defined in the present report). Unfortunately, we cannot specify causal directionality, i.e., if the hypothesis is supported, we cannot be certain which of the two following assertions is true:

1. Use of participatory media lessens anomie.
2. Individuals with low anomie will be more likely to use participatory media.

In addition, there can be an interaction effect between the two situations. However, at the least, we can establish, for the first time, whether any relation obtains between usage and anomie as a prolegomenon to further research. (Further research, e.g., might be of this order: individuals are scaled for anomie, then one group is given a special program involving easy access to and high utilization of participatory media; after some time the two groups are remeasured to see whether the utilization of participatory media by the experimental group had any effect in lowering anomie.)

The Srole Scale

The Srole anomie scale is composed of five statements. The respondent is asked either to agree or disagree with each item. Only the agreement responses are scored. Thus the respondent's total score falls in a range from 0 to 5. The higher the numerical score the greater the amount of anomie demonstrated by the respondent. The scale consists of the following questions.

1. In spite of what some people say, the lot of the average man is getting worse.
2. It is hardly fair to bring children into the world with the way things look for the future.
3. Nowadays a person has to live pretty much for today.
4. These days a person does not really know who he can count on.
5. There's little use in writing to public officials because they often are not interested in the average man.[a]

Approximately 61 percent (60.5 percent) of the sample scored low on anomie, agreeing with two or fewer statements (see table 7.1,, and this conventionally has served as the dividing line. Of the 36.6 percent of the sample who scored from 3 to 5 on the Srole anomie scale, the largest grouping (15.2 percent) were in agreement with four anomie statements. The highly anomic group (five agreements) accounted for 7.9 percent of the total sample.

Anomie and Letters to the Editor

Anomie was found to be inversely related to writing letters to the newspaper, according to table 7.1.[b] The mean anomie score of those who had written one or

---

[a]Robinson and Stover, 1969:172.

[b]This compares favorably with the sample taken by Leo Srole, the creator of the scale, in Springfield, Mass., when 61 percent of the respondents scored 2 or less, *ibid.*

Table 7-1
Anomie Score of Respondents and Writing Letters to a Newspaper

	Yes		*No*	
0–agree	23	25.8	197	22.4
1–agree	18	20.2	171	19.5
2–agree	28	31.5	166	18.9
3–agree	8	9.0	126	14.4
4–agree	7	7.9	144	16.4
5–agree	5	5.6	74	8.4
Total	89	100.0	878	100.0

Note: *N* excludes incomplete and no response cases.

more letters to the editor was 1.70 while those who had not written a letter had a mean anomie score of 2.08. The distribution in table 7.1 indicates that those who scored 2 or less on the Srole scale account for approximately 79 percent of letter writers compared to 61 percent of the non-writers. Approximately 23 percent of writers and 39 percent of non-writers scored high on anomie, with three or more.

Anomie and "Sound Off"

The mean anomie score of respondents who had sought help from "Sound Off" was higher than those who had not, but only slightly higher, 2.23 compared with 2.04. The distribution comparison in table 7.2 indicates small overall differences as well. Hannigan's study of the "Sound Off" client suggested similar results, with the complainant scoring 3.64 on Seeman's powerlessness scale compared with an average figure in an Ohio City of 2.70 (Hannigan, 1972: 112).

Table 7-2
Anomie Score of Respondents and Ever Contacted "Sound Off"

	Yes		*No*	
0–agree	8	21.1	213	22.9
1–agree	7	18.4	182	19.5
2–agree	8	21.1	186	20.0
3–agree	5	13.2	130	14.0
4–agree	9	23.7	142	15.3
5–agree	1	2.6	78	8.4
Total	38	100.1	931	100.1

Note: *N* excludes "No Response" cases.

Anomie and the Call-In Show

The mean anomie score of individuals who had used a call-in show was 1.98 compared with 2.06 for those who had not, an insignificant difference. The comparison of the distributions (table 7.3) indicated no substantial differences either.

Summary Statement on Anomie

When the distributions of the three tables are compared, we find that approximately 79 percent of all newspaper letter writers, 61 percent of those contacting "Sound Off," and 62 percent of those calling "Open Line" shows are classified as low anomie. Thus, the only participation channel which indicates a *general* difference on this variable is newspaper letters. However, since past research has shown that there exists a relationship between the use of the mass media and social status, this differential usage by social status may in fact suggest that some of the variation in our findings can be accounted for by the same factor. Some *is* accounted for by occupational status, per se. Occupational status (as measured by the Blishen scale) was therefore introduced as a convenient control measure. As is indicated in table 7.4, lower status respondents who had written a letter to the editor had a mean anomie score of 1.8, while those who did not had a score of 2.7; middle status letter writers had a score of 1.5, while those who did not had a score of 1.7. Upper status letter writers score 1.5 while those who did not write scored 1.4. Thus, it can be seen that for lower and middle statuses, those who wrote were lower in anomie than those who did not write.

Radio call-in shows, when controlled for occupational status, followed the earlier pattern, with little difference, as seen in table 7.3. The controlled analysis of "Sound Off" suggests in general a higher anomie score for users than non-users. However, in view of the fact that it involved the smallest sample size and that cells were very small, the validity of results from this cross-tabulation may be questioned, yet it suggests the possibility – for future research follow-up – that the newspaper ombudsman serves a group whose alienation from society includes an inability to cope on their own or, alternatively, highlights the failure of society to provide training and channels that would permit them to use their own resources to solve their problems. In this, they appear to resemble the subsample of high anomie individuals who use radio call-in shows for problem-solving purposes, as described below.

Although the measures of central tendency do not indicate any difference between callers and non-callers, a more detailed analysis of the callers may reveal interesting differences in the functions performed by the call-in show for individuals who vary in anomie. This test of the function of a participatory channel is possible in the case of radio only because of the large size of the

Table 7–3
Anomie Score of Respondents and Calling the Open Line

	Yes		No	
0–agree	46	24.0	176	22.6
1–agree	40	20.8	149	19.1
2–agree	33	17.2	161	20.7
3–agree	28	14.6	107	13.7
4–agree	33	17.2	119	15.3
5–agree	12	6.3	67	8.6
Total	192	100.1	779	100.0

Note: N excludes Incomplete and "No Response" cases.

Table 7–4
Anomie and Usage of Participation Channels Controlled by Occupational Status

	Lower Status		Middle Status		Higher Status	
	Yes	No	Yes	No	Yes	No
Letters to Editor	1.8	2.7	1.5	1.7	1.5	1.4
"Sound Off"	3.1	2.7	2.0	1.7	2.0	1.3
Call-In Shows	2.6	2.7	1.6	1.7	1.3	1.3

Note: N excludes all incomplete and "No Response" cases.

subsample, 190 callers who indicated *why* they had called. (The subsamples of letter writers and "Sound Off" clients were too small to permit such an analysis.)

First of all, a content analysis of the reasons for the call was performed and three general functions were discerned.

1. Some individuals called to give their *opinions* on a topic.
2. Some individuals called for *informational* purposes, i.e., to make announcements, to request information, or to provide information.
3. Some individuals called for *problem-solving* purposes, i.e., the radio host was asked to help them to solve a problem dealing with other individuals, organizations or firms.[b]

As has been pointed out elsewhere, radio shares with the letters to the editor column some functions, primarily the *opinion expression* function. In addition, it provides an important channel for the exchange of information and to some extent provides an ombudsman function. It was hypothesized that the anomie

---

[b]These three categories were achieved through collapsing the "Purpose of the Calls"

scores of those whose calls tapped the ombudsman function would be, like the users of "Sound Off," higher than those who used the show for informational or opinion expression purposes. The results were as follows.

Persons who called to give their *opinions* ($N = 74$) had a mean anomie score of 1.86. Persons who called for *informational* purposes ($N = 96$) had a mean anomie score of 1.85. Persons who called for *problem-solving* purposes ($N = 20$) had a mean anomie score of 2.60.

It thus appears to be clear that the different channels not only serve different purposes and different audiences, sociologically, but that certain participatory channels provide a service needed by some parts of the population who can be identified in terms of social-psychological dimensions. Electronic participatory channels also offer a service which individuals who otherwise have difficulty coping appear to need and use.

In summary, then, the data in this section suggest the potential importance of certain kinds of relationships to mass media for engagement in society and that what we call "participatory" media channels are not the same for all individuals. Table 7.5 has been constructed to make it possible to assess each medium comparatively.

The data are suggestive, if not conclusive. They suggest, as one interpretation, that use of letters to the editor either reflects a group well-integrated in modern society, possibly one which knows how to use certain societal mechanisms for asserting oneself or "blowing off steam," or alternatively that those who customarily use such means become, through this process, protected from alienation or anomie. The radio call-in show does not discriminate on this dimension, nor does the use of "Sound Off," although the detailed analysis of purposes served by radio suggests the differential functions performed for different kinds of individuals.

Stimulus to Participate

Earlier, in the review of past literature, the point was made that we can distinguish analytically between the issue *why* some individuals participate and *what stimulated them to participate.* The data in the present report aid us in understanding why in the sense that socioeconomic data on individuals and topic distributions tell us something about the underlying factors that may predispose one or another group to participate, using a given kind of channel for expressing themselves on a given subject. The question of the proximate stimulus cannot be as easily confronted. It should be added that although the distinction can be made analytically, empirically, in the actual world of events, it is more difficult to separate these factors. It will be recalled that the earlier cited study by Foster and Friedrich done in the 1930s asserted that "The newspaper itself conveyed the most frequent stimulus to write to the editor. The majority of published

Table 7-5
Anomie Rating of Users of Various Participatory Channels

Classification			Anomie Rating
Yes – Letters to Editor			1.70
Yes – Radio Call-in Show			1.98
. Opinions		1.86	
. Information		1.83	
. Problem Solving		2.60	
No – "Sound Off"			2.04
No – Radio Call-In Show			2.06
No – Letters to Editor			2.08
No – Any of three channels			2.10
Yes – "Sound Off"			2.23

letters referred to news items, other letters or to editorials." Thus, it is not the mere *presence* of a medium with a feedback channel, but rather some content that elicits communicative behavior on the part of the reader or listener, according to the earlier study.

In his paper, "Access to Information: A Position Paper on Communication Channels and Social Change" (1970), Singer suggested that in planning communications systems for the future one should not be misled by optimistic technological determinists that the mere provision of multiple channels would assure their use. The behavior of the medium or channel (previous content), in a sense, will help to determine participation, not the mere availability of facilities. While the present data do not aid us in understanding this issue, findings in separate researches help throw light on the matter. Content analysis of an approximately 23 percent subsample ($N = 234$) of 1,020 letters to the editor of the *London Free Press* and of 3,224 taped-off-the-air calls to London radio stations in 1970 revealed that approximately one-third of the letters and approximately one-half the calls were in response to previous stimuli in the newspaper or on the radio program (see table 7.6), (Singer and Cameron, 1971).

It is interesting to note that approximately four times as many radio calls were stimulated by previous calls by other listeners as letters that were stimulated by past letters. Thus, it would appear that a major reason for calling the radio show is in fact located in the stimulating effect of other members of the audience. The analogies that have been made comparing radio call-in shows to small town telephone party lines may not be so far off.

Another point that might be made in line with the "blowing off steam" function various authors have discussed is that radio may be capable of originating, more often, the tension that subsequently, through a call, is cathartically drained off, whereas the newspaper letters column may present for *its* audience a means of discharging tensions which are more often present due to other factors in social life. If one takes this analysis farther, then it might also

Table 7-6
Stimulus Factor for Letters to Editor and Call-In Radio Shows

	Letters to the Editor		Call-In-Radio Shows	
Self-Initiative	150	64.1	1,593	49.4
Stimulated by Media Content	{ Letters 23 { Editorials 20 { Articles 41	9.8 8.5 17.6	{ Calls 1,319 { Commentary 39 { Other Media D.J. 273	40.9 1.2 8.5
	TOTAL 84	35.9	TOTAL 1,631	50.6
Total	234	100.0	3,224	100.0

Note: All letters and calls that referred explicitly or implicitly to a previous letter, article, editorial, past call, radio commentary or statement by the radio host were coded "Stimulated by Media Content."

explain (under the assumption that anomie score reflects a state of tension resulting from existence in mass society) why newspaper letter writers score lower on the anomie scale. These are possible explanations, which, unfortunately, the present research cannot confirm or deny.

References

Hannigan, John A. "The Newspaper Ombudsman and the Redress of Consumer Complaints." Master's thesis, University of Western Ontario, 1972.

Robinson, John P., and Shaver, Philip R. *Measures of Social Psychological Attitudes.* Ann Arbor: Institute for Social Research, University of Michigan, 1969, p. 172.

Singer, Benjamin D. "Access to Information: A Position Paper on Communication Channels and Social Change." Presented at the Telecommunications Seminar, Department of Communications, Ottawa, May 16, 1970.

Singer, Benjamin D., and Cameron, Andrew D. "The Radio Call-in Show." An unpublished study, 1972.

_____ . "Letters to the Editor." An unpublished study, 1971.

8

The Information Center

The objectives of the present research are to study the pattern of usage of a typical information center in order to discern the kinds of needs expressed, the channels used to link individuals to the center and the relationship of the two factors to the sociological characteristics of clients. In addition, some information is available on the pattern of action of the center in response to inquiries.

The Users of the Information Center

In this section we shall present a brief description of the kinds of individuals who called upon Information London for services. The description is based upon the sex, age, and education data gathered.

The fact that all societies are stratified in terms of the characteristics felt important within specific societies has served as the major rationale for the existence of much of today's sociology. Perhaps the most universal dimensions of status by which individuals are stratified are age and sex. Following closely behind is an often diffusely described phenomenon called "social class," which has been defined in a number of different, often confusing ways. In general, there is agreement that in Western society, occupation, income, and education help to define one's class position and are criterion variables, singly or in combination, for the social scientist's attempt to rank individuals.

Particularly since the time of Marx, students of the sociology of knowledge are fond of pointing out that "consciousness" is strongly linked to one's position in the social system; one's position, of course, depends primarily on social class but also on other status characteristics such as sex and age. Although the most general use of the term "consciousness" embraces quite centrally the notion of one's world view or, more specifically, ideology, the increasing emphasis of much of North American sociology during the past decade has been on the results of being located in a specific knowledge system which results from being located in a specific place in the social system. The point that has been made is that one's social position will be related to one's needs for assistance, and one's fund of knowledge about present sources of information and help; and it follows from this that approaching a central information and referral service will reflect lack of success in finding out things or, alternatively, may simply represent for some a continued aggressive persistence.

Since one's position in society is so dependent upon the factors of sex, age and social class, we shall be attempting to discern how these sociological characteristics are related to the use of information centers. Social class is most often defined by occupation and/or by income. However, because of the sensitivity of the second question and the stronger relevance for the study of information centers of education (information centers are essentially a cognitive concern), we have chosen to ask about this factor since it is highly related to other social class criteria.

Sex

According to the Census of 1966, 51.5 percent of the population of London, Ontario, was female and 48.5 percent was male. The data on Information London's clientele indicates that 65.2 percent of clients were female and 34.8 were male (see table 8.1).

There are several possible explanations for this difference (approximately 30 percent female overrepresentation among Information London clientele). One is that females, by virtue of a different pattern of socialization and different contact with the working world, may be less knowledgeable about channels which males are more familiar with due to their involvement with the working world.

A second explanation may involve the fact that females have a greater range of responsibilities, e.g., child care, which may mean that they as a population have more concerns that refer to outside organizations. Finally, in many cases, they may be assuming tasks which the male cannot do because he is at work.

Any or all of these explanations may be among the factors accounting for the higher usage by females.

Table 8-1
Sex of Information London Respondents Compared with Census Sex Data for 1966

| | Sample | | Census | |
	Number	Percentage	Number	Percentage
Male	656	34.8	94,294	48.5
Female	1,230	65.2	100,122	51.5
Total	1,886	100.0	194,416	100.0

Age

A comparison of the age distribution of Information London clients with that of the Census for 1966 indicates interesting differences (table 8.2)

The youngest segment of users of Information London services is under-represented by approximately half, compared with census statistics and this probably reflects their relative lack of involvement in the world of responsibility. At ages 20-29 the sample indicates considerable overrepresentation (32.4 percent compared with 18.8) and it may be because, when the individual acquires the major responsibilities of the adult world — employment, marriage, and a family — he will have greater need for information on services related to these concerns. At ages 30-39 there continues to be higher usage, 24.3 percent compared with census figures of 16.5, but as the individual enters his most successful years vocationally and as his children mature, ages 40-49, his needs go down as reflected in the data, 14.8 percent compared with 16.0 percent census figures. At ages 50-59 there continues to be underrepresentation, 8.7 percent compared with 11.5 percent for Census figures, as is true for the age period 60-69, 6.1 percent compared with 7.6 percent.

There is striking underrepresentation for ages 70-79 (1.5 percent compared with 5.1 percent for the census) as is true for 80 and over (0.3 percent compared with 2.1 percent for the Census).

Although we have looked at age-patterned usage as a factor reflecting needs associated with different family cycle patterns, it is also possible that age may be associated with higher degrees of experience with services in the past, or lack of knowledge of such new institutions as Information London or even increasing apathy which results in fewer services being used by the individual.

Table 8-2
Age of Information London Respondents Compared with Census Age Data for 1966

Years of Age	Sample		Census	
	Number	Percentage	Number	Percentage
10–19	160	11.9	34,520	22.4
20–29	435	32.4	28,850	18.8
30–39	325	24.3	25,400	16.5
40–49	199	14.8	24,565	16.0
50–59	117	8.7	17,707	11.5
60–69	81	6.1	11,694	7.6
70–79	20	1.5	7,781	5.1
80 and Over	4	0.3	3,155	2.1
Total	1,341	100.0	153,672	100.0

Note: N excludes 40,744 persons who are less than 10 years of age.

Education

The most striking finding of table 8.3 is the very substantial underrepresentation of the lowest education group, primary school or less, among clients of Information London when compared with the 1966 census. The users in the sample amount to 8 and 25 percent (primary school, some high school) compared with 34 percent in the population, according to the Census. At the high school graduate level, there is substantial overrepresentation among users, 37.8 compared with 23.8, and this trend becomes more pronounced as one climbs the educational ladder: some college, 12.3 percent compared with 3.7 percent; graduates and above, 17.0 percent compared with 4.7 percent.

Another way of examining the educational data is to compute usage by individuals drawn from different educational levels on a per thousand population basis. Table 8.4 provides these computations. There is a striking difference, with university graduates and postgraduates using information services approximately fifteen times as much as individuals with primary school education.

The argument can be made that in the five years between the 1966 census and the present research, the educational level shifted upward (unfortunately, census data for the latter time are not yet available); however, any upward shifts that may have occurred would in fact tend to exaggerate the differences shown here.

Summary of the Social Profile

Females, young adults, and the well-educated were the most frequent clients of Information London for the time period studied. Several explanations were suggested for the high proportion of females and of young adults. The apparent under-use of such facilities by the aged and less educated individuals suggests in addition that more will have to be done to acquaint these groups with information centers and to facilitate their usage. It is in fact those who possess the least education who probably are in greatest need of the kinds of services which information centers can provide, as Kahn pointed out.

The Inquiries

Identifying the Callers. There are two basic classes of callers: the individual calling on his own behalf, or others calling in his behalf. Table 8.5 indicates that approximately 85 percent of the calls come from individuals or relatives of individuals and that the other 15 percent come from outside agencies or friends. Although there is no distinction made in the coding between "self" and "relatives," staff members of Information London estimate that nine out of ten calls are from the individual concerned.

Table 8–3

Education Level of Information London Respondents Compared with Census Education Data for 1966

	Sample		Census	
	Number	Percentage	Number	Percentage
Primary School or Less	97	8.2	35,969	34.0
Some High School	293	24.7	35,733	33.8
High School Graduate	449	37.8	25,185	23.8
Some College	146	12.3	3,850	3.7
College Graduate and Postgraduate	202	17.0	4,964	4.7
Total	1,187	100.0	105,701	100.0

Table 8–4

Inquiries Per Thousand Population By Educational Level

	Number of Inquiries	Population	Rate Per Thousand for 3-Month Period
Primary School or Less	97	35,969	2.70
Some High School	293	35,733	8.20
High School Graduate	449	25,185	17.83
Some College	146	3,850	37.92
College Graduate and Postgraduate	202	4,964	40.69

Table 8–5

Source of Initial Contact

	Number	Percentage
Public–Self & Relatives	1,591	84.6
Health, Welfare, Recreation	114	6.1
Public–Other	67	3.6
Other Government Services	39	2.1
Professional Associations	36	1.9
Business & Labor	33	1.7
Total	1,880	100.0

Thus it becomes clear that the information center for the most part is linked directly to the individual seeking help or information for himself.

Channels Used. Information centers such as Information London depend overwhelmingly on the telephone for inputs from clients. Table 8.6 indicates that 93.5 percent of contacts made were by telephone with another 6.5 percent occurring through personal interviews. Other studies of this factor may suggest higher proportions of personal interviews where neighborhood centers are included in the population sampled. Information London, however, corresponds more closely to the community information center inasmuch as it is the only such organization in London and is located in the downtown area.

Type of Inquiry. Broadly speaking, there are two major kinds of inquiry. These are described as Service Inquiries or Address-Phone-Name. As is indicated in table 8.7 approximately 28 percent of all inquiries request the kind of information that is often conveniently located in various directories and other printed sources or which may be known personally to staff members. But, nearly three-quarters of all inquiries require discretion, the assessment of the request, perhaps more research and a determination of the service needed.

Category of Inquiry. As table 8.8 indicates, the range of information requested is very broad, even broader than the categories used by staff in their records system, which in itself is a "collapsed" schema into which requests are fitted. The most frequent categories are leisure, representing approximately 17 percent of inquries, followed by general and then consumer categories, with approximately 12 percent each. With the exception of the rank order indicated in table 8.8, no pattern can be discerned; later in this report, we shall examine the categories of inquiries in relationship to social characteristics in an attempt to discern whether certain groups tend to cluster around specific information needs.

Disposition. The two most basic kinds of service provided consist of the provision of information only – such as amount of monthly old age pension or the name of the lieutenant governor of Ontario – or direction, i.e., the client is given the directions for contacting the correct agency or service for his needs

Table 8-6
Channel Used

	Number	Percentage
Telephone	1,787	93.5
Interview	124	6.5
Total	1,911	100.0

Table 8–7
Type of Inquiry

	Number	Percentage
Service Inquiry	1,375	72.3
Address, Phone, Name	527	27.7
Total	1,902	100.0

Table 8–8
Categories of Inquiry

	Number	Percentage
Recreation – Vacation	320	16.8
General	225	11.8
Consumer	220	11.5
Other	175	9.3
Financial	150	7.8
Health (Physical & Mental)	128	6.7
Landlord & Tenant	125	6.5
Employment/Vocational	113	5.9
Accommodation	100	5.2
Legal	92	4.8
Education	70	3.7
Government Service Information	47	2.5
Home Services	39	2.0
Child Welfare	37	1.9
Pollution	35	1.8
Adjustment (Family, Individual)	27	1.4
Dental Care	5	0.3
Immigration	1	0.1
Total	1,909	100.0

(see table 8.9), with the first category representing approximately 47 percent of contacts and the second 39 percent.

Following in frequency are advice and guidance only, approximately 9 percent, and "Information obtained by Inf. London," where Information London contacts the agency or service and gets information on behalf of the client.

Summary on Inquiries

In summary, Information London is a center which works directly with the concerned client for the most part. The channel used for contact between client

Table 8–9
Disposition of Inquiries

	Number	*Percentage*
Information Only	875	46.6
Direction (Caller to Contact)	730	38.9
Advice & Guidance Only	158	8.5
Information obtained by Inf. London	68	3.6
Other	23	1.2
Referral or Direction Back	12	0.6
Referral (Inf. London made Contact)	10	0.5
Service Performed	2	0.1
Total	1,878	100.0

and the information service overwhelmingly is the telephone. The most prevalent kind of inquiry requires skill, knowledge, and discretion on the part of the staff rather than involving the mere transmission of patent information from printed sources. Leisure, other, and consumer inquiries are most frequent. Disposition of cases most often involves giving information rather than selection of an appropriate other agency, followed by directions for contacting an agency for service, and advice and guidance.

The Inquirer and His Inquiry

We have, in an earlier section, examined some social characteristics of clients of Information London, and in Chapter 4 we surveyed what happened when they contacted the information center. In this section we wish to bring these data together to aid in better understanding the way in which information centers serve specific social groups. We shall therefore examine the relationships between social characteristics of clients and the inquiries which they make.

Male-Female Differences in Contact Channels

Male-Female Differences in Contact Channels. Table 8.10 indicates that males contact Information London via interviews approximately twice as high a proportion of the time as females (approximately 10 percent compared with 5 percent). Although the overall use of personal interview still represents a small proportion of the interaction between Information London and clients, nevertheless this pattern of differences may suggest that females more often would use the personal interview mode if they were less homebound by responsibilities and possible lack of transportation.

Table 8–10
Channels Used by Males and Females

	Male		Female		Total	
Telephone	591	90.4	1,172	95.3	1,763	93.6
Interview	63	9.6	58	4.7	121	6.4
Total	654	100.0	1,230	100.0	1,884	100.0

Male-Female Differences in Types of Inquiry. Females slightly more often (74 percent) than males (70 percent) make service inquiries requiring more extensive information intervention by staff, when compared with straight name-address-organization information (see table 8.11).

Male-Female Differences in Categories of Inquiry. As is indicated in table 8.12, there are no substantial differences between males and females in categories of inquiry. Females call more often about child welfare, home services, and consumer problems and pollution, and considerably more often about health problems and services. Males call more often on employment and vocational problems, landlord and tenant problems, legal matters, recreation and vacation questions.

Male Female Differences in Disposition of Inquiry. As was true for categories of inquiry, there is little difference in the action supplied by Information London for males and females, in fact, the differences are even smaller, with the single exception that "Information obtained by Information London" is slightly higher (4.1 percent) for females than males (2.8 percent) (see table 8.13).

Age Differentials in Usage Patterns

Age and Channels Used. As is indicated in table 8.14, the youngest category of individuals (10-19 years) as well as individuals in the 50-59 age range least often use the telephone, instead preferring the personal interview (approximately 11 and 15 percent). Individuals in the 30-39 age range most often use the telephone

Table 8–11
Inquiry Types by Males and Females

	Service Inquiry		Address-Phone		Total	
Male	453	69.9	195	30.1	648	100.0
Female	907	73.9	320	26.1	1,227	100.0
Total	1,360	72.5	515	27.5	1,875	100.0

Table 8–12
Male-Female Differences in Categories of Inquiry

	Male		Female		Total	
Accommodation	35	5.4	62	5.0	97	5.1
Adjustment	8	1.2	19	1.5	27	1.4
Child Welfare	7	1.1	28	2.3	35	1.9
Employment & Vocational	46	7.1	65	5.3	111	5.9
Financial	56	8.6	94	7.6	150	8.0
Health	32	4.9	95	7.7	127	6.8
Home Services	12	1.8	27	2.2	39	2.0
Landlord & Tenant	49	7.5	75	6.1	124	6.6
Consumer	67	10.3	152	12.4	219	11.6
Education	22	3.4	48	3.9	70	3.7
Legal	37	5.6	55	4.5	92	4.9
Other	50	7.6	119	9.7	169	9.0
General	86	13.2	136	11.1	222	11.8
Dental Care	1	0.2	4	0.3	5	0.3
Gov't Service Info.	19	2.9	27	2.2	46	2.4
Recreation & Vacation	117	17.9	196	15.9	313	16.6
Immigration	1	0.2	0	0.0	1	0.1
Pollution	7	1.1	28	2.3	35	1.9
Total	652	100.0	1,230	100.0	1,882	100.0

Table 8-13
Male-Female Differences in Disposition of Inquiry

	Male		Female		Total	
Referral	2	0.3	8	0.7	10	0.5
Direction	250	38.7	473	39.2	723	39.0
Referral or Direction Back	6	0.9	6	0.5	12	0.7
Advice & Guidance Only	52	8.1	105	8.7	157	8.5
Information Only	310	48.0	550	45.5	860	46.4
Other	8	1.2	15	1.2	23	1.2
Information obtained by Information London	18	2.8	49	4.1	67	3.6
Service Performed	0	0.0	1	0.1	1	0.1
Total	646	100.0	1,207	100.0	1,853	100.0

Table 8-14
Age and Channels Used

	Telephone		Interview		Total	
10–19	143	89.4	17	10.6	160	100.0
20–29	398	91.3	38	8.7	436	100.0
30–39	313	96.6	11	3.4	324	100.0
40–49	188	94.5	11	5.5	199	100.0
50–59	100	85.5	17	14.5	117	100.0
60–69	74	91.4	7	8.6	81	100.0
70 and Over	23	95.8	1	4.2	24	100.0
Total	1,239	92.4	102	7.6	1,341	100.0

Table 8-15
Age and Types of Inquiries

	Service Inquiry		Address Phone		Total	
10–19	108	68.8	49	31.2	157	100.0
20–29	314	72.4	120	27.6	434	100.0
30–39	231	71.5	92	28.5	323	100.0
40–49	149	75.3	49	24.7	198	100.0
50–59	85	73.3	31	26.7	116	100.0
60–69	59	72.8	22	27.2	81	100.0
70–79	16	80.0	4	20.0	20	100.0
80 and Over	0	0.0	2	100.0	2	100.0
Total	962	72.3	369	27.7	1,331	100.0

(approximately 97 percent of the time). There does not appear to be a strong discernible pattern, therefore, by age.

Age and Type of Inquiry. There is an unclear association between age and type of inquiry (see table 8.15); for example, the youngest category (10-19 years)

Table 8-16
Age and Categories of Inquiry

	10–19		20–34		35–59		60+		Total	
Other–General	33	20.6	114	18.7	88	19.0	22	21.4	257	19.2
Recreation–Vacation	39	24.4	110	18.0	84	18.1	13	12.6	246	18.4
Accommodation	19	11.9	83	13.6	53	11.4	12	11.6	167	12.5
Consumer	10	6.3	68	11.1	67	14.4	22	21.4	167	12.5
Financial	5	3.1	50	8.2	39	8.4	12	11.6	106	7.9
Health	10	6.3	37	6.0	32	6.8	9	8.7	88	6.6
Employment-Vocational	18	11.2	31	5.0	24	5.2	1	1.0	74	5.5
Legal	9	5.6	34	5.6	26	5.6	1	1.0	70	5.2
Education	9	5.6	21	3.4	12	2.6	0	0.0	42	3.1
Family Services	1	0.6	20	3.3	12	2.6	0	0.0	33	2.5
Gov't. Info. Services	4	2.5	19	3.1	11	2.4	1	1.0	35	2.6
Home Services	2	1.3	9	1.5	12	2.6	6	5.8	29	2.2
Pollution	1	0.6	15	2.5	4	0.9	4	3.9	24	1.8
Total	160	100.0	611	100.0	464	100.0	103	100.0	1,338	100.0

least often (approximately 69 percent) use Information London for service inquiries and most often use it for address and phone service; on the other hand, the age category 70-79 most often (80 percent) make service inquiries. Otherwise, ages 20 through 69 are relatively similar.

Age and Categories of Inquiry. Table 8.16 utilizes compressed age categories for the purpose of noting discernible age variation with categories of inquiry; the original table (see Appendix) is 7 by 18 cells. As can be noted, inquiry categories are related to age. The highest proportion of inquiries concerning leisure is in the 10-19 age bracket and, in general, descends with age. Consumer inquiries rise sharply with age, from 6.3 percent in the 10-19 age bracket to 21.4 in the 60-plus age grouping. There is a consistent association between financial inquiries and age, from 3.1 percent at 10-19 years to 11.6 percent in the highest age bracket. Employment-vocational inquiries are at their height in the 10-19 age category with 11.2 percent and drop to 1 percent in the highest age category. There is a dropoff in legal inquiries after age sixty. Education inquiries are highest in the 10-19 bracket and diminish steadily with age. Family services contacts are at their height in the 20-34 bracket. Home services rise consistently with age.

This section has documented a clear and strong relationship between age and the kinds of inquiries brought to Information London.

Age and Disposition. The strongest association between age and kind of service rendered ("disposition") is in the category *direction* — where the client needs to know whom to contact and the name and phone number of an appropriate agency or service. Table 8.17 (with age categories condensed as in the previous table) indicates a positive association with age in requirements of this kind of service; on the other hand, the category *advice and guidance only* drops off with age as does *information only*.

Education Differentials in Usage Patterns

Education and Channel Used. There is no consistent pattern linking educational level to channel used to contact Information London. As table 8.18 indicates, individuals with primary school education only used personal interviews most, approximately 9 percent; followed by individuals with some university education, approximately 8 percent; and some high school and university training, approximately 8 percent. The middle education category, high school graduate, used the telephone most, with approximately 3 percent of such contacts being by personal interview.

Table 8-17
Age and Disposition

	10-19		20-34		35-59		60+		Total	
Referral	1	0.6	3	0.5	2	0.4	1	1.0	7	0.5
Direction	52	32.9	227	37.6	200	44.0	44	43.1	523	39.6
Referral or Direction Back	1	0.6	4	0.6	1	0.2	0	0.0	6	0.5
Advice & Guidance Only	15	9.6	56	9.3	35	7.7	6	5.9	112	8.5
Information Only	80	50.6	292	48.3	201	44.2	46	45.1	619	47.0
Other	0	0.0	6	1.0	0	0.0	1	1.0	7	0.5
Information Obtained by Information London	9	5.7	15	2.5	16	3.5	4	3.9	44	3.3
Service Performed	0	0.0	1	0.2	0	0.0	0	0.0	1	0.1
Total	158	100.0	604	100.0	455	100.0	102	100.0	1,319	100.0

Table 8-18
Education and Channel Used

	Telephone		Interview		Total	
Primary School	78	90.7	8	9.3	86	100.0
Some High School (Gr. 9-11)	274	93.5	19	6.5	293	100.0
High School Graduate (Gr. 12-13)	437	97.5	11	2.5	448	100.0
Some University	135	91.8	12	8.2	147	100.0
University and Postgraduate	188	93.5	13	6.5	201	100.0
Total	1,112	94.6	63	5.4	1,175	100.0

Table 8-19
Education and Type of Inquiry

	Service Inquiry		Address-Phone		Total	
Primary School	60	70.6	25	29.4	85	100.0
Some High School	208	71.5	83	28.5	291	100.0
High School Graduate (12-13)	321	71.8	126	28.2	447	100.0
Some University	105	72.9	39	27.1	144	100.0
University & Post-graduate	146	72.6	55	27.4	201	100.0
Total	840	71.9	328	28.1	1,168	100.0

Education and Type of Inquiry. Table 8.19 indicates that there are no education-linked differences in types of inquiry.

Education and Category of Inquiry. The majority of inquiry categories are not associated with educational level; however, there are discernible differences with respect to recreational, accommodations, consumer services, financial services and legal help and information (see table 8.20).

As will be noted, the higher one's educational level, the more likely one is to make an inquiry dealing with leisure (recreation, vacation, etc.). However, this relationship is reversed for accommodations, consumer services, financial services, and legal help, with the lower educational groupings making a higher proportion of inquiries in these areas.

It becomes clear, then, that information centers such as London's serve the different social needs of varied social groupings and that further development

Table 8–20
Education and Category of Inquiry

	Primary School		Some High School		High School Graduate		Some University		University & Postgrad.		Total	
Other–General	14	16.3	42	14.3	94	21.0	36	24.5	47	23.4	233	19.8
Recreation–Vacation	10	11.6	44	15.0	90	20.1	28	19.1	31	15.4	203	17.3
Accommodation	16	18.7	44	15.0	48	10.7	19	12.9	14	7.0	141	12.0
Consumer	10	11.6	46	15.8	58	12.9	13	8.8	22	10.8	149	12.7
Financial	12	13.9	35	11.9	28	6.3	9	6.1	10	5.0	94	8.0
Health	5	5.8	19	6.5	38	8.5	8	5.4	13	6.5	83	7.1
Employment-Vocational	3	3.5	14	4.8	22	4.9	7	4.8	12	6.0	58	4.9
Legal	5	5.8	15	5.1	23	5.1	6	4.1	12	6.0	61	5.2
Education	3	3.5	8	2.7	13	2.9	6	4.1	13	6.5	43	3.7
Family Services	2	2.3	8	2.7	8	1.8	5	3.4	12	6.0	35	3.0
Gov't. Service Info.	3	3.5	6	2.1	14	3.1	3	2.0	8	3.9	34	2.9
Home Services	2	2.3	9	3.1	7	1.6	1	0.7	4	2.0	23	1.9
Pollution	1	1.2	3	1.0	5	1.1	6	4.1	3	1.5	18	1.5
Total	86	100.0	293	100.0	448	100.0	147	100.0	201	100.0	1,175	100.0

Table 8–21
Education and Disposition

	Primary School		Some High School		High School Graduate		Some University		University & Postgrad.		Total	
Referral	0	0.0	5	1.8	2	0.5	0	0.0	0	0.0	7	0.6
Direction	37	43.0	122	42.6	163	37.0	60	41.1	82	41.0	464	40.0
Referral or Direction Back	0	0.0	3	1.1	2	0.5	0	0.0	1	0.5	6	0.5
Advice & Guidance Only	9	10.5	26	9.1	29	6.5	14	9.6	19	9.5	97	8.4
Information Only	37	43.0	123	43.0	224	50.8	66	45.3	93	46.5	543	46.9
Other	0	0.0	0	0.0	2	0.5	3	2.0	2	1.0	7	0.6
Information Obtained by Information London	3	3.5	7	2.4	19	4.2	3	2.0	3	1.5	35	3.0
Service Performed	0	0.0	0	0.0	0	0.0	0	0.0	0	0.0	0	0.0
Total	86	100.0	286	100.0	441	100.0	146	100.0	200	100.0	1,159	100.0

of facilities to emphasize the requirements of specific social groups requires a consistent program of evaluation of these needs.

Education and Disposition. There is no marked pattern of differences in the kind of disposition made by educational level of clients (see table 8.21). However, individuals with high school or above tend to require information only slightly more often.

9 Summary and Conclusions

This book has concerned itself with two of our society's mass feedback modes, the mass media and the information center. The picture thus provided helps inform us concerning the strengths, the functions, the similarities and the differences in these institutions, many of which are relatively new. A summary and discussion of findings concerning each of the two major kinds of feedback modes, the mass media and the information center, will be presented along with some comments and recommendations.

Mass Media Feedback

The paucity of research dealing with the question of mass media feedback systems led to the posing of a number of questions.

The first has dealt with the issue of the kinds of mass media channels available in a typical North American city which make it possible for individuals to not only participate in the process of opinion formation, but to also inquire and to seek help. How widespread is actual usage, and what kind of division of labor exists among the media channels?

The feedback channels made available by mass media in London, Ontario, included letters to the editor columns, the "Sound Off" column of the *London Free Press* and the call-in radio shows in London. Approximately 9 percent of the adult population had ever written a letter to the editor and 6 percent had had a letter published. The newspaper ombudsman, "Sound Off," had been contacted by 4 percent of the sample and slightly more than half had had their problem solved as a result. Surprisingly, 20 percent of individuals had telephoned a radio show.

How regularly newspaper letters were sent was gauged by the answer to how often during the past two years the individual had written. Only 27 percent sent more than one. On the other had 38 percent of individuals who had called a phone-in show had done it more than once. There may, in fact, be more "regulars" who listen to be stimulated to call and who are multi-issue callers rather than selectively using the channel for fulfilling a previously held need to express themselves on a specific issue. The unpublished content analysis data referred to in "Other Factors" indicated that 50 percent more often individuals who used radio call-in shows did so as a response to a stimulus within the medium, something which had been aired already, as compared with newspaper writers who had written in response to a previously printed item.

The second question asked: 'Who has access to such channels? No general survey has ever previously been fielded that answers the question, 'Who uses which channels for what purposes?' The question '*Who*' refers to the socio-logical characteristics of users."

The sociological characteristics of interest include sex, age, family income, and education. The data clearly reveal that males are overrepresented and females underrepresented among letter writers. Males were also overrepresented among users of "Sound Off." Among individuals who had called a radio station, on the other hand, females were overrepresented, a fact attributed in part to the time of day the programs are broadcast. Males, then, for the most part, dominate the printed media and females the broadcast channels.

There were no substantial differences in the ages of channel users, with the median age for letter writers and non-letter writers being 38; for "Sound Off" clients, 36; with nonusers, 38; but there was a larger difference in median age of radio show callers to non-callers, 40 and 36; the youngest and oldest categories were underrepresented and the middle-aged were overrepresented by nearly 20 percent.

There were greater differences on the variable education, however, with substantial overrepresentation among the highest educated groups in letter writing and, conversely, substantial underrepresentation among the lowest education groups. The user of the "Sound Off" column was lower in education, while the radio show caller tended to more often be in the middle education category, with the very low and very high education groups underrepresented.

More often than not, the family income of the letter writer and the individual who called radio shows was higher than that of those who did not use these channels; on the other hand, the family income of the client of "Sound Off" was slightly lower than that of the non-user.

Another factor examined was that of success in getting a letter published and here it was found that the successful were older, more often male, higher in income, and were more likely to have sent fewer than three letters. Interestingly enough, education made no difference. These findings confirm earlier assertions that suggested that the editor as gatekeeper might screen out certain members of society, however lower education is not a factor in the screening process.

The occupational status controlled analysis of participation and anomie revealed that lower and middle status individuals who wrote to newspapers were less anomic, hinted that users of the newspaper ombudsman might be more anomic and indicated little if any difference in the use of radio call-in shows. The use of certain kinds of participation channels does appear to be related to one's feeling of integration in society.

The third question raised in this research was: "How do the various channels – printed and electronic – compare in carrying out relevant social functions? What kind of process is the communications linkage that is established?" The answer to the first point will be answered by summarizing the findings concerning the purpose and content of the interaction; and the second seeks to appraise the stimulus factor.

The content topics of newspaper letters and radio call-in shows indicate, first of all, that the highest category of communications in both cases is politics, government, and social issues of the day, with a slightly higher proportion being found in letters compared to telephone calls. Letter writers are more concerned with education, with local issues, and with mass media. Callers are more concerned with animals, complaints of a personal nature, or dealing with products or services. In general, the topics of the radio callers suggest a concern that is more immediate, of a more personal nature; and those in the newspaper appear to concern issues of longer range importance, more separated from the immediate needs of the individual. Radio performs more of an ombudsman function as well. This appears to be borne out when one examines the purpose of the letter or call. Approximately four times as many individuals used the newspaper column to give an opinion on a topic than was true for the radio caller. Nearly six times as frequently, radio callers used this channel to get information than was true for letter writers, and nearly five times as often to give information. Radio callers also used this channel for lost and found notices (not mentioned at all by letter writers) and to get help on some problem.

When these channels, therefore, are compared with the newspaper ombudsman, "Sound Off," whose most prevalent category was consumer problems, followed by government problems, it appears that radio call-in shows actually combine the functions performed by the letters to the editor column and the newspaper ombudsman in being both an opinion forum as well as offering personal help in information seeking and problem solving.

The off-the-air study indicates that radio shows depend more heavily on stimulation by the host and past calls than newspaper letters are stimulated by other content or past letters. The analysis of the pattern of usage helps us to identify a set of distinct usage groups from within the population who use such shows rather than suggesting a homogeneous group who fit one stereotype of the callers, e.g., the semi-literate lunatic fringe. Actually, the most prevalent usage-group identified in this study is the *utilitarian* group who use such shows to gain information or help or to offer information or help.

These findings help to answer our question which called for a comparison of feedback institutions in terms of carrying out relevant social functions. Newspaper letters to the editor columns generally serve individuals more preferentially located in the social structure and function essentially as a means for presenting their viewpoints more often generated apart from the stimulus of the medium. The newspaper ombudsman serves a less preferentially located audience, is highly specific in purpose, and aids individuals in relationships with organizations with whom they have had communication difficulties and lack of success in gaining their ends. The column accomplishes the task for the individual. Radio serves the most heterogeneous audience of all — the closest approximation, in fact, to the population — is more diffuse in function, serving to stimulate those who are listening to express their opinions on subjects more often generated by the program, and serves an ombudsman function as well.

Conclusions

Existentialist philosopher Karl Jaspers has written that communication is "the universal condition of man's being. It is so much his comprehensive essence that both what man is and what is for him are in some sense bound up with communication" (Jaspers, 1955:79). Along with this communication-centered view of man's psyche, we consider the common plaint of critics of mass society, that this psyche is on the receiving end of a cultural apparatus which directs messages to him: a one-way process that does not give modern man a chance to answer back. One model for the role of mass media in a true mass society has been provided by the late C. Wright Mills.

Technical conditions of the media make a selection of speakers necessary and, by determining the low ratio of speakers to hearers, limits the chances to answer back . . . Public opinion then consists of reactions to what is presented in the formal media of communication; personal discussion does not affect the opinion formulated; and each man is an isolated atom reacting alone to the orders and suggestions of the monopolized mass media. (Mills, 1963:582)

We have not yet arrived at that state, according to Mills; however, many critics of mass communications systems would argue that we are enroute. This should be viewed in the context of the "communications transactional view" of modern societies taken by such authorities as Deutsch and Meier, which asserts that messages define the boundaries of organizations, are surrogates for trips, and that changes in patterns of human interaction to reduce communication stress are required to improve the welfare of urban residents. (Deutsch, 1966: Meier, 1962). How well, we can ask, do communications institutions in our society serve as true centers for transactions initiated from below, for the individual living in a complex society?

Optimists relying on the new technologies being perfected in communications suggest that access to public communications will increase for the individual and this presumably will cause a surge in the proportion of two-way communication when compared with one-way message patterns. The functions performed by closed channel television and multi-channel cablecast, tape recorders the linkage of telephone to radio and other developments will result in, among other things, the elevation of the public opinion process to parity with opinions generated at the top of the social structure, a new sense of efficacy for the common man in his attempts to actualize himself in Jaspers' sense, and perhaps, flowing from this, a lessening of the feeling of alienation or disaffection.

It is difficult, however, to assess the potential of such communications technologies for two-way communication without first establishing the meaning of such two-way communication — the social and psychological functions they may perform — and this we have attempted to do through an analysis of the usage patterns and kinds of users employing present mass two-way channels. We have found three functions now being performed for users: opinion presentation, information seeking and provision and the ombudsman-interventionist function.

One of the three channels studied, newspaper letters serves individuals more preferentially located in the social system, who also appear to be the least anomic. They are used to disseminate opinions more often of a catholic nature. The radio show serves the most people and the most typical kinds of individuals. whose opinions deal with more parochial and personal concerns and more of the content is generated by the program itself; but it also serves a two-way information function and as an ombudsman for more anomic individuals who need help. The newspaper ombudsman is the most specialized of the three channels and provides direct intervention for individuals who can't cope otherwise.

In addition to defining the present usage and users, this research suggests that some of the channels are operating in a closed system manner in the sense that many issues are raised within the boundaries of the system of broadcaster-to-audience, letters-column to user. This is in part true for the opinion presentation usage, more so with radio, less so with newspaper letters. The ombudsman and information functions do not share in this.

The study of channels such as these can help to provide a sensitive picture of the state of the population, an index of important problems within the system, at the least. By their very presence, such institutions suggest the need within our society for more institutions devoted to the provision of information and coping aid which would be readily available by telephone for large segments of the population. At present such channels are limited in the sense that some opinion is generated within the system and much that comes from users does not go beyond the subsystem. Thus, it neither informs policy makers of a state of the system — in the sense that other social indicators are used — nor is there any assurance that effective action will be taken either on specific issues or classes of events: that opinions expressed and needs indicated will result in changes in the system.

One way, then, in which such quasi-closed, two-way systems can be "opened up" would be for policymakers to use such two-channels in a social indicators fashion, i.e., employ regular monitoring of such channels in order to assess a state of opinion as well as patterns of unmet needs, particularly from individuals less preferentially located. While it can be argued that this method of making it possible for feedback to have an effect at the top may produce biased results — in the sense that only certain segments of the population use certain channels — nevertheless, with time, as opinions, quests for information and help became transformed into further concerned inquiry higher up, more individuals would find it efficacious to use such channels in a manner in which they would be most effective so that such institutions might ultimately come to approximate a true *vox populi.*

The Information Center

The purpose of the research on the Information Center is to help to understand the role of a new "knowledge institution," the information center. It has been suggested that people with the greatest needs have the lowest access to vital information and this study has been an attempt to investigate the needs and patterns of usage by present clients of an information center through analysis of certain social characteristics of users, and the pattern of their usage and to highlight any relationships between these. This kind of information may help to provide guidance in planning further information center services, particularly in view of the fact that information center personnel feel the need to develop better techniques, and such may involve information storage and communicating machines.

Concerning the social characteristics of users, the data reveal that males, the very young and the elderly, and those with less formal education are underrepresented among users with respect to their numbers in the population. As to the channels used, it has been found that the telephone is used most of the time and that information centers are linked directly to individuals rather than through secondary sources; and that the large majority of users require more extensive information than that routinely available by standard sources such as directories. Thus, the amount of human labor necessary is high.

Inquiry subject matter is most often recreational, general, consumer, and financial; but contrary to some suggestions, rather than high levels of intervention or advocacy, most inquiries are processed with the provision of information alone.

Cross-tabulation analysis reveals few relevant differences with respect to sex of the user. Males are slightly less likely to use the telephone in their contacts, females slightly more often require more than routine information services, but there are few substantial male/female differences in categories of information or in disposition of the request.

Age provides greater variation than sex. While people of different ages contact the center in the same manner, the youngest and oldest age categories are different with respect to categories of inquiries, with the younger clients more often inquiring concerning leisure and older clients more often needing consumer, financial, and home service information, while information related to employment and vocation drops with age.

Educational level was also related to categories of inquiry, with individuals in lower levels requiring more help concerning accommodations, consumer services, and financial and legal information.

The data presented here, then, do document the fact that present usage of the information center is skewed: there is under-usage by males, the young, the elderly and lower educational groups, some of them the very individuals who need the most help. This may be a function of the kinds of promotion campaigns undertaken by such centers, the newness of the center (which could help determine the kind of people who would have heard of it), or it may even be that the information center, as it is presently operated, is simply another mechanism by which already high copers can extend their coping capabilities. If we also assume the kinds of inquiries made are an accurate reflection of needs, then we find that the pattern of needs is related to such social characteristics as age and educational level.

If the findings of this research can be generalized, there may be important implications for future planning. At present, the center studied services approximately four inquiries per annum per hundred population (examination of reports of other centers suggests that this figure is fairly representative). If there were to be an increase in usage by groups now underrepresented, overwhelming demands would be made on information center staffs. If, for example, the usage of the lower educational groups were brought up to the same proportional amount as the highest educational levels, inquiries would un- doubtedly increase between 300 and 400 percent, to somewhere between 12 and 16 inquiries per hundred population per annum.

Information centers may find themselves on the horns of a twin dilemma. One of the implications of the present findings is that more "outreach" attempts should be made to increase usage by those who are believed to be in greatest need (e.g., the lower educational groups, the elderly, the very young); but in doing so, such would be generating a new problem as a result of the increase in volume of inquiries which may require solution by the adoption of more information storage and transmission facilities and the software that accom- panies such.

Some Concluding Remarks

A distinguished contributor to the study of communications, Harry Skornia, has remarked that we are still forced to rely on nineteenth century media to communicate with the leaders of our institutions. And Boulding's portrait of the role of feedback in determining the kind of system in which we live —

authoritarian or democratic – has added chilling emphasis to the object of the research presented in this book. A democratic society, as it enlarges and becomes characterized as a mass society, can also become transformed without volition or consciousness of its state, into an undesirable society. The vigorous maintenance of true feedback systems geared to the kinds of functions revealed in this book, will help to preclude that kind of development.

In addition, it is necessary that the complete cycle of the feedback process be completed, that the kinds of patterns of needs revealed by such institutions be studied and taken into account in determining policy on a national basis.

Earlier in this book I pointed out the problems we face in attempting to make relevant contact and in making our voices heard as part of the public opinion process. Yet the subject of this study has, in fact, been the existent major mass institutions which serve that very purpose. There is, of course, no contradiction. These institutions exist; they exist, however, for certain people; some of these institutions possess common or overlapping functions, and some are more accessible. Their study should guide us in further improvement and development of present institutions and perhaps even suggest models of a new and more unorthodox nature that meet the needs of individuals in a large-scale society.

References

Deutsch, Karl W. *The Nerves of Government.* New York: The Free Press, 1966.

Jaspers, Karl. *Reason and Existence.* New York: Noonday Press, 1955.

Meier, Richard L. *A Communications Theory of Urban Growth.* Boston, Mass.: Massachusetts Institute of Technology, 1962.

Mills C. Wright. "Mass Media and Public Opinion." In I.L. Horowitz, ed. *Power, Politics and People: The Collected Essays of C. Wright Mills.* New York: Ballantine Books, 1963.

WMCA Sample Editorials

Promise Them Anything, But Give Them Nothing

Broadcast 8 times
December 13-14, 1964

For 22 months, WMCA: Call for Action has fought for better housing enforcement as one way to wipe out slums.

One hot day last August, Mayor Wagner admitted that Call For Action was right in its accusation that dozens of different city agencies all had their fingers in the housing pie and they were making a mess of it.

So the Mayor gave his City Administrator some orders, and one of them was to set up a single telephone number for all housing complaints, as the very first step toward centralized housing enforcement.

We are now in a wintry December and even that first step hasn't been accomplished. We still don't have that single phone number, slum tenants still get a run-around and housing enforcement is still a mess.

From August to December is a long time to wait for a phone number. How can slum tenants hope to escape from their misery when the city's motto seems to be: "Promise them anything, but give them nothing."

Housing # 44

Broadcast 8 times
December 27-28, 1964

Our city's housing laws are enforced in total administrative chaos. Because of this, hundreds of hardened slumlords get away with criminal exploitation of the poor.

For almost two years, WMCA: Call For Action has said this and made several recommendations to the city, including the creation of a single housing enforcement agency.

The city has done nothing to bring order out of its chaos, except to study the problem. Our recommendations have been under study by the Columbia Law School and the City Administrator for months and months. A preliminary report is to be made to the Mayor before December 31st — less than one week away.

We hope this means action — and soon — for the slum victims of our city government's chaos. We hope it's not just another case of "Promise them anything, but give them nothing."

Housing # 73

Broadcast 8 times
February 21-22, 1966

About fifty thousand slum tenants are being cheated out of decent housing by a ring of real estate speculators whom we call "Slumlords, Incorporated." WMCA has exposed some of them by name.

We have shown how they make fortunes, while their buildings fall apart. Big profits are being made out of the misery of thousands of men, women and children.

To correct this, WMCA is sponsoring bills to make slumlords personally responsible for repairing their rotten buildings. You can help get the WMCA bills passed.

Send a post card to "Slumlords," WMCA, New York City, 10017. Tell us you support the WMCA bills and we will see that the lawmakers get your message. That's "Slumlords," WMCA, New York City, 10017.

Appendix 1B — Topics of
Letter Writers
(Coding Breakdown)

1. Politics, government, and social issues of the day

   environment
   religion
   long hair, youth
   racial problems
   women's lib
   politics
   nationalism
   laws and policy
   strikes
   employment
   alderman invitation

2. Local issues and services

   local service
   traffic hazard
   bus, taxi drivers
   recreation-Doidge Park

3. Education

4. Sports and Special Events

   sports
   special events
   bingo

5. Mass Media

   media
   offensive material
   coverage
   Needham
   advertising
   magazine article

6. Animals

7. Complaints of a personal nature or dealing with products or services

   personal problems
   products & services
   mistreatment

8. Health and Housing
    health
    housing

9. Other and Miscellaneous
    music
    organizations

Appendix 1C — Sound Off
(Coding Breakdown)

1. Consumer Problems
   billings
   product complaints
   contractural obligations
   firm
   landlord-tenant

2. Government Problems
   tax
   pollution
   city services
   legal problems

3. Other
   neighbor problems
   family problems
   information

4 Media problems
   media complaint

5. Health, Education and Welfare Problems
   medical service

6. Employment problems
   employer

Appendix 1D — Open-Line Callers
(Coding Breakdown)

1. Politics, government, and social issues of the day
   laws & policies
   politics
   strikes
   militant
   Irish struggle
   war measures /FLQ
   environmental problems
   prejudice
   religion
   drugs

2. Local Issues and Services
   local services
   police
   road conditions
   fraud, theft
   parking
   meter reading
   L.T.C.
   accidents

3. Education

4. Sports & Special Events
   special events
   sports events
   Grand Theatre

5. Mass Media
   contest
   disasters, storms
   location
   media
   weather
   poem
   historical facts

6. Animals
   animals
   Humane society

7. Complaints of a personal nature or dealing with products or services

personal problems
wallet
customs & etiquette
truck drivers
baby sitting
camp
products and services
insurance
car dealers
model train

8. Health and Housing

landlord-tenant
cooking, diet
health
housing
wheelchair
chemicals

9. Other & Miscellaneous

organizations

1. Name   (last)   (first)

2. What was the last grade completed (or highest educational level you reached)?   Your spouse?

3 What is your religion?

   Protestant
   Roman Catholic
   Other — Christian
   Jewish
   Other — non-Christian
   None

4. What is your main occupation?   (If not working, what was your last job or occupation?)

5. What is your family's total yearly income from all sources? (Show respondent a cue card.)

   a. Less than $3,000
   b. $3,000-$4,999
   c. $5,000-$6,999
   d. $7,000-$9,999
   e $10,000-$14,999
   f. $15,000-$19,999
   g. $20,000-$24,999
   h. $25,000 and Over
   i. Refuse to answer, don't know
   j. Not working, no income

6. Which newspapers do you get daily? (Specific titles needed). (Get=Receive, Buy or Subscribe to).

7. What is the main reason why you buy — 1st paper,   then 2nd paper, 3rd etc., (Circle appropriate number below for each newspaper).

   Local coverage
   National news
   International news
   Editorial features
   Sports
   Other

8 Have you ever written a letter to the letters-to-the-editor column in a newspaper?
Yes
No
Don't Know

9. Was the letter ever published?

10. If Yes, how many letters have you written in the past *two* years?

11. How many letters were published?

12. What was each of these letters about?

13. Have you ever contacted "Sound Off" in the *London Free Press*?
Yes
No

14. If *YES*, over what issue?

15. What action resulted, if any?

16. Have you ever called the Open Line show?
Never
Once
A few times
Quite often
Every day

17. Why did you call this program?

18. We would like to ask if you AGREE or DISAGREE with the following statement(s):

In spite of what some people say, the lot of the average man is getting worse.
Agree
Disagree

It is hardly fair to bring children into the world with the way things look for the future.
Agree
Disagree

Nowadays a person has to live pretty much for today.
Agree
Disagree

These days a person does not really know who he can count on
Agree
Disagree

There's little use in writing to public officials because they often are not interested in the average man.
Agree
Disagree

Appendix 2 — The Off
the Air Study

Content Coding Analysis

The content of each call was analyzed and used to generate general categories which follow:

Content of the Calls

1. *Entertainment, recreation, sports, hobbies, special events & meetings:*
   Recipes — how to make wine, puff balls
   Sports — football and baseball games
   Skating, hockey, skiing
   Art exhibitions
   School shows
   Suppers — pancake, fall, bean festivals
   Meetings — Pollution, Drug Abuse

2. *Health, welfare, medical & social services:*
   Medical facilities — hospitals, doctors, nurses, clinics
   Health insurance
   Organized facilities for those in need — United Appeal
   Allowances — youth and old age pensions
   Unemployment Insurance
   Funerals and cremations

3. Consumer:
   Consumer goods and products — umbrellas, rural mail-boxes, new toothpaste (any good)
   Repairs and repairmen — high costs
   Ticket raffles and sweep stake tickets
   Defective goods and services — Metro Colour Studio Finance Companies

4. *City services — (Transportation & Post Office):*
   PUC — garbage men, road conditions, city dump
   Parking meters
   Licenses — pilots, drivers
   Hitch-hikers
   London bus service — raise in prices
   New postal rates
   Pornographic mailings
   Postmen — put mail in boxes instead of finishing their routes

5. *Social Problems – (police, crime, discrimination, & Quebec):*

Stolen goods
Tickets
Traffic Hazards
Punishment system – jails and judges (should not charge drunks)
Immigrants, old people, Indians, kids with long hair
Working wives and mothers
Women's Liberation
Hate literature
Kidnapping – FLQ
Bilingualism
Separatists

6. *Provincial & federal administration, laws, politics, & politicians:*

Laws – gun and liquor (Octoberfest)
Licenses – fishing, marriage, drivers
Department of Transport
Day light saving time – should have a vote
Government planning
Indians' rights
Canadian currency and inflation
Present government – luxury can't afford
Farmer subsidizes
Armed Forces
NDP, CPL
Robarts
Trudeau – trips, marriage
MP's raises

7. *Media & Advertising:*

Media in immediate area –
    CFPL – TV and Radio
    CKSL
    CJOE
    London Free Press
Advertising – misadvertising
Content of media – books, TV, radio

8. *Employment, vocations & labor:*

Unions
Strikes and demonstrations
Further job training or retraining

Lack of jobs — students, etc. (working mothers give up jobs to a student for the summer)

9. *City politics, administration & urban planning:*

City manager — does the city need one
New city hall
City Council and the Mayor (has a sauna bath)
City by-laws — clearing of side-walks
Parking — downtown area, Doidge Park-St. Joseph Hospital issue
Land fill areas
Roads — open or closed

10. *Youth Culture:*

Drop-in-center
Fashions — midi, mini, maxi
Morals and drugs
Gives thanks to young people who help others

11. *Animals*

Licenses — costs, where to get them
Special shows
Vets
Specific problems — cat caught in car fender

12. *Personal & interpersonal relations:*

Birthday
Reads poem
Jogs every day
Husband forgot something
Problems with neighbors
London — friendly or unfriendly
Trying to get in contact with another person

13. *Education:*

Sex education in the schools
Bilingual schools
Teachers — dismissal of Terrance Fenn
Registration — kindergarten

14. *D.J.:*

Comment on him personally
Praise or take exception to his remarks
Correct information he has given

15. *Miscellaneous:*

Lightning — go up to sky or down to earth
Odors — mustly smell out of trunk, paint
Day light savings time — when does it start
Definitions

16. *Housing, accommodation, landlord & tenant:*

Rental problems — rebates, evictions, heat, leases
Accommodation — vacations, permanent

17. *International problems:*

Communism
Trade Relations
United States — investments, buying up land

18. *Pollution:*

Garbage — dumping on private property
Environmental — hydro — hot water into the Great Lakes
Pollution Probe
Odors — plant outside St. Marys

19. *Pest problems & suggested cures:*

Pests — wasps, bees, skunks, fruit flies

20. *Religion:*

Church services and sunday schools — cancelled or moved
Spiritualism
End of the world is coming

21. *Taxes:*

Income, capital gains, sales, property, educational

**1971 Record Forms — Definitions (Revised
Effective June 1, 1971)**

Boxes in Upper Left-Hand Corner. Identification numbers have been allocated to each information centre for purposes of computerized data processing. These may be already printed on the record form, but if not, they must be written on *each* record form.

1. *Office Hours* (A) — For enquiries received during the *normal* hours of operation for *your* centre (i.e., if you normally operate during evening hours, you would consider calls received during those hours as office hours.)

2. *After Hours* — Enquiries received outside your normal operating hours, whatever time this may be.

Initial Contact (B)

NOTE: Calls relayed by switchboards (United Appeal, after hours answering services, city halls, etc., should be noted under "Contact By (C)".

10. *Public — Self & Relatives* — Indicates calls from an individual about a problem he himself has or that a relative of his has. (This would include individuals from #'s 12-15 when they are calling on behalf of themselves or a relative.)

11. *Public — Other* — Calls from an individual on behalf of a neighbor, friend, or fellow employee. (Includes individuals from #'s 12-15 calling on behalf of a neighbor, friend, or employee.)

12. *Health, Welfare, Recreation* — Calls from government departments of health, welfare, and recreation about one of their clients or other business. Calls from hospitals and voluntary health, welfare and recreation services about a client or other business. (This includes ethnic services but excludes those that do not provide social services.)

13. *Other Government or Public Supported Services* — Includes such services and departments as:

    a.   Federal Departments of
         Immigration
         Indian Affairs

Canada Manpower
Unemployment Insurance Commission
Veterans

b. Ontario Departments of

Justice
Corrections
Education
University Affairs
Emergency Services
Ontario Housing Corporation
Labor (including Human Rights Commission)
Legal Aid Plan
Provincial Secretary
Workmen's Compensation Board

c. Municipal Departments of

Building
City Clerk
Boards of Education, Schools
Housing
Libraries
Planning Police

d. Also includes

Consulates
C.Y.C.
C.B.C.

14. *Business, Labor* — Indicates calls from business firms (an employer, the personnel department, industrial nurse) on behalf of an employee or other business.

— Calls from unions, including enquiries from unions directed through United Appeal or U.C.F. May be on behalf of union member or other business.

— Calls from news media (other than C.B.C. which is # 13).

— Calls from commercially operated schools, nurseries, nursing homes, boarding homes, etc.

15. *Professions and Associations*— Calls from individuals who are professionals (doctors, lawyers, nurses, psychiatrists, psychologists, therapists, etc.) on behalf of a client or other business.

— Calls from Church councils, boards, ministers and workers. *Associations* — Calls from ethnic associations (except those mentioned in # 12); professional associations (except those mentioned in # 12);

civic organizations such as Association of Women Electors or whatever; Board of Trade; non-profit clubs; service clubs; community or citizens groups or projects.

16. *Neighborhood Information Centre* — Calls from neighborhood information centres asking for assistance in handling an enquiry.

Contact by (C)

20. Telephone
21. Interview
22. Correspondence
23. *Answering Service* — Indicates calls relayed by telephone answering service

Type of Enquiry (D)

This section is used to indicate whether an enquiry requires an assessment (and therefore a degree of skill and knowledge) on the part of the information centre staff person handling the call, or whether it is simply a straightforward request for factual information.

30. *Service* — Indicates that skill in assessing the request and in determing the appropriate service is required. Indicates also that knowledge of community resources, functions, and policies is required, including general community information, trends, etc.

31. *Address, Phone, Name Only* — Indicates enquiries where a specific telephone number, address, or organization is requested; or where the name of a specific person in an agency is requested (i.e., "Who is the principal of the local public school?").

Special Groupings (E)

Where the following situations are a factor in requesting information or service, check only if applicable and you can identify the caller as being in one of the following groups:

40. *Aged* — 60 years and over.

41. *Handicapped* — Physically or mentally handicapped, of any age.

42. *Youth* — 16 to 21 years.

43. *Immigrants* — As a guideline, up to 5 years residence in Canada.

44. *Migrants* — Refers to persons from other parts of Canada outside the metropolitan or local area who come without prior arrangements for adequate employment or training and accommodation, or whose plans break down prior to their becoming established.

45. *Language Problem* — Indicates client is unable to communicate in English (or French, where French is working language) and requires:
   a. an interpreter
   b. information provided in his own language, or
   c. resource providing service in his own language

46. *Welfare Recipient* — If so stated by the client either directly or indirectly.

47. *Preschoolers* — Indicates enquiries where the problem is around a preschool-aged child.

Category of Enquiry (F)

50. *Accommodation* — With or without service and care (excluding child placement), includes:
   — Housing (rooms, houses, apartments)
   — Hostels, residences, hotels
   — Homes for the aged and nursing homes (permanent)
   — Boarding homes
   — Offering accommodation

51. *Adjustment* — Family or individual (excluding budgeting and debt counslling, # 54; vocational counselling, # 53; and educational counselling, # 59).
   — Premarital counselling
   — Marriage counselling
   — Family counselling
   — Unmarried parents counselling
   — Individual counselling
   — Support of wife and children

52. *Child Welfare* — Indicates enquiries about care of child in or out of own home, usually because parents are working. Includes enquiries about:
   — Day nurseries
   — Boarding homes
   — Sitters (live-in or by day)
   — Camps (as a form of· day care rather than for education or recreation purposes)
   — Legal adoption, neglect, foster care

53. *Employment & Vocational* (Other than rehabilitation due to physical or mental condition, which would be # 55)
   - Vocational counselling
   - Employment placement
   - Apprenticeship programs
   - Adult training or retraining

54. *Financial* — Indicates enquiries about government pensions, insurance, allowances, assistance, including assistance for:
   - Payment of gas, hydro, rent
   - Payment of glasses, dentures, drugs, and other health needs
   - Clothing, furniture
   - Moving expenses
   - Debts and loans including budgeting help
   - Transportation for indigents
   - Etc.

55. *Health — Physical and Mental*
   - Health services
   - Mental health services
   - Retardation services
   - Physical or mental rehabilitation
   - Home care (where therapy or V.O.N. is the primary need)
   - Treatment and convalescent care (active treatment hospitals, convalescent hospitals, chronic hospitals, nursing homes for temporary care
   - Wheelchair, bed, crutches on loan

56. *Home Services* — Indicates enquiries around the following types of services:
   - Home care (for a person who qualifies for a Home-maker Service through the Home Care Program)
   - Companion for elderly person, invalid, etc.
   - Sitter (for elderly or invalids, including baby sitters)
   - Mother's Helper (where the mother is in the home)
   - Housekeeper
   - Home-maker
   - Meals-on-Wheels
   - Maintenance chores (e.g. someone to cut the grass, do the shopping, fix the screens, etc.)

57. *Landlord and Tenant* — Indicates problems between landlord and tenant, such as:
   - Tax (or rent) rebate

- Rents
- Deposits and leases
- Heat
- Maintenance and repairs

58. *Consumer* – Indicates enquiries or complaints pertaining to standards, merchandising or advertising of goods and/or services, including professional services.

59. *Education* – Indicates enquiries about education, including:
    - Educational counselling
    - Formal or informal education
    - Day or night classes
    - Extension classes at universities and colleges (degree or non-degree)

NOTE: This is meant to be a broad definition and in some cases there will be doubt as to whether an enquiry is around "education" or "recreation and vacation" (#65). Generally speaking, things like swimming classes, craft classes, and other such instruction readily associated with recreation or hobbies, should be included in #65 "recreation and vacation". (In addition, it is not particularly important at this point to split hairs over whether an enquiry about basket weaving classes would come under "recreation" or under "education".)

60. *Legal* – Indicates enquiries where professional legal information, advice or action is required, including Legal Aid.

61. *Other* – Indicates anything not already covered in numbers 50-67, including such matters as:
    - Offering volunteer services or facilities
    - Volunteer service needed

62. *General* – Indicates enquiries about services in a specific field or area (e.g., services for the aged; services in a geographical area such as the Mountain in Hamilton, the Glebe in Ottawa, or Earlscourt in Toronto).
    - Name, address, or telephone, where reason is not given or not pertinent
    - General agency information (not related to an individual need)

63. *Dental Care* – Indicates enquiries about dental care, whether or not there is a financial problem.

64. *Government Service Information* – Indicates enquiries about government (municipal, provincial, federal) services not covered in numbers 50-67, or enquiries about government services where it is clear that the enquiry is not related to a specific need or problem.

65. *Recreation and Vacation* — Indicates enquiries about recreation or vacation, including:

— YMCA and other organized instruction in athletic or sports activities

— YMCA and other organized instruction in arts and crafts

66. *Immigration and Citizenship* — Indicates enquiries about immigration or taking out Canadian Citizenship.

67. *Pollution* — Indicates enquiries where pollution is the main concern of the caller:

— Reporting a polluter

— Offer to help in anti-pollution campaign

— Etc.

Multi-Problem (G)

70. *Multi-problem* — Where an enquirer has more than one problem (often related to the main problem) and for which help is suggested in addition to the major problem as shown in numbers 50-67.

Urgent (H)

73. *Urgent* — This is additional to and refers to any one of the problems in numbers 50-67, where the urgency of the situation demands immediate service or action by an organization or other resource.

Disposition (J)

This indicates what the information center actually does with the enquiry — what action the information center takes.

80. *Referral* — Where information centre makes contact with an agency or resource.

— Information centre discusses individual enquiry with agency or resource which then accepts responsibility for offering the needed service.

— In some cases the resource or agency accepts responsibility for contacting the enquirer; in other cases the enquirer is given the name and telephone number of the person and he is expected to make the call himself.

81. *Direction* — Where the enquirer himself contacts agency or resource needed.

— Caller is given name and telephone number and any necessary guidance in approaching the agency or service (e.g., hours of operation, appropriate office or person, help with phrasing the enquiry, etc.)

— Alternate suggestions may also be given (e.g., community contacts, advertising, etc.

82. *Referral or Direction Back* — Where appropriate action (disposition) is a referral or direction back to an agency or other resource to which the enquirer is known of with which he has had recent contact.

83. *Advice and Guidance Only* — Where no referral or direction is appropriate or possible (numbers 80, 81, 82, 86, 87 already are understood to contain advice and guidance in those dispositions). Discussion of alternative plans and providing brief counselling.

84. *Information Only* — Where factual information only is given, requiring no selection as to the appropriate agency or service.

85. *Other* — Where a person refuses service or hangs up.

— Disposition incomplete for some reason (e.g., insufficient information given and enquirer to call back but doesn't, information centre unable to call back at pay phone, or person gone, etc.)

— No service available and no alternative suggested.

— Information requested not known and no referral or direction or alternative suggestion made.

86. *Information Obtained by Information Centre* — This is to be used when an information centre, on behalf of an enquirer, has to get or provide information that should be readily available to anyone capable of getting that information. This may be where an enquirer expresses dissatisfaction with information he obtained, or has expressed some other difficulty involved in obtaining information from an agency or service he contacted.

— Also where because of previous experience the information centre knows the enquirer will not be able to get the needed information on his own and therefore takes the initiative in getting the information for him.

NOTE: This does not refer to cases where the enquirer has not been able to get needed information because of a language problem, mental retardation, etc.

87. *Service Performed* — Where the information centre performs a service such as helping to fill out forms providing interpreter services, acting as an escort service, etc.

— Does not include simple distribution of pamphlets or application forms where no help to the enquirer is given in filling out the form.

— Includes interpreting services whether requested by an agency or by the enquirer.

— Assistance in obtaining information where there is a language problem.

Needed Service Doubtful or Not Available (K)

88. *Needed Service Doubtful or Unavailable* — (NOTE: This is additional to and refers to any one of # 80-87 above.)

— Refers to situations where, in the judgment and experience of the information centre, service to meet the reasonable needs of the enquirer is doubtful or unavailable because of a long waiting list, cost to the enquirer, inadequacy of the service needed, or other factors.

Service Consulted, Referred or Directed to (L)

This section indicates the sole or major agency or organization to which an enquirer is referred or directed in # 80, 81, or 32. Also indicates those organizations where the disposition is # 86 (i.e., information itself is difficult to get or unavailable).

90. *Municipal Welfare* — Refers to municipal welfare office, often known as Department of Social Services.

— Where municipal welfare office also performs other social services within same office, these referrals and directions are also to be indicated here.

91. *Ontario Department of Social and Family Services* — Includes contacts with the following branches and services of the Department:
    — Family Benefits (provincial welfare)
    — Child Welfare Branch
    — Day Nurseries Branch
    — Homes for Aged Branch
    — Vocational Rehabilitation Branch
    — Family Services Branch

92. *Canada Manpower* — Canada Manpower Centres for employment, counselling, retraining, etc.

93. *Unemployment Insurance* — Unemployment Insurance Commission main and walk-in offices.

94. *National Health and Welfare* — Department of National Health and Welfare, including contacts re:
    — Canada Pension Plan
    — Old Age Security
    — Guaranteed Income Supplement
    — Family Allowance
    — Family Assistance
    — Youth Allowance
    — Other contacts with this Department

95. *Immigration and Citizenship* — Indicates referral, direction, or consultation (as per # 86) to Federal Immigration offices.
    — Also refers to Canadian Citizenship Courts.

96. *Public Health* — Public health departments, units, or district offices (both local and provincial), including mental health department.

97. *Doctors and Medical Academies* — Refers to doctors in private practice or providing medical supervision through a hospital or clinic.
    — Refers to medical academies where the information centre contacts them to ask for assistance in getting a doctor for an enquirer.

98. *Ontario Housing* — Ontario Housing Corporation including contacts re:
    — Applications
    — Maintenance offices
    — Community relations officers

99. *Senior Citizens Housing* — Includes senior citizens apartments and residential hotels, room rental service, boarding homes.
    — *Excludes* homes for the aged and nursing homes.

100. *Hostels — Adults* — Temporary or emergency hostel accommodation for adults over 21 years.

101. *Hostels — Youth* — Temporary or emergency hostel accommodation for youth between 16 and 21 years.

102. *FSA's* — Family counselling agencies including only Family Service Association, Catholic Family Service and Jewish Family & Child Service.

103. *CAS's* — Children's Aid Society and Catholic Children's Aid Society.

104. *Legal Aid* — Refers to Legal Aid Plan and Lawyer Referral Service.

105. *Landlord Tenant Bureau* — Refers to Landlord — Tenant Bureau, where it has been established.

106. *Metro Day Nurseries* (Toronto) — Refers to Metro Toronto Department of Social Services Day Care Services Unit.

107. *Missions, Churches* — For emergency assistance, counselling, etc., but excluding senior citizens clubs.

108. *Senior Citizens Clubs* — (Including those under church auspices).

109. *Other* — All other organizations, departments, etc., not covered by numbers 90-116.

110. *Ontario Department of Labor* — Includes contacts to the various services and branches of this Department, such as:

— Employment Standards Branch (minimum wages, overtime payments, etc.)
— Women's Bureau (equal pay for equal work, etc.)
— Industrial Training Branch (apprenticeship programs, other upgrading programs)
— Human Rights Commission
— Workmen's Compensation Board

111. *Consumer Service* — Refers to consumer departments and organizations such as:

— Ontario Department of Financial and Commerical Affairs (Lotteries Branch; Ontario Securities Commission; Superintendant of Insurance; Consumer Protection Bureau; Registrar of Real Estate and Business Brokers; Registrar of Used Car Dealers; Registrar of Collection Agencies, Mortgages Brokers, and Bailiffs; Upholster and Stuffed Articles Branch; Companies Branch).
— Federal Department of Corporate and Consumer Affairs.
— Better Business Bureau
— Canadian Consumers Association.

112. *Recreational or Educational Facility* — Indicates local schools, school boards, universities, colleges, etc.

— YMCA's, YWCA's, YM-YWHA's, Community Recreation Centres, etc.

113. *Other Health Service* — Indicates V.O.N., Red Cross, Dentists, medical clinics, optometrists.

114. *Other Municipal Service* — Indicates any other municipal service not already covered in numbers 90-116.

115. *Other Provincial Service* — Indicates any other provincial service not already covered in numbers 90-116.

116. *Other Federal Service* — Indicates any other federal service not already covered in numbers 90-116.

Appendix 3A —
Disposition (Coding
Breakdown)

1. *Information Only:*
   — where factual information only is given, requiring no selection as to the appropriate agency or service.

2. *Direction (caller to contact):*
   — where the enquirer himself contacts the agency or resource needed — caller is given name and telephone of agency or service.

3. *Advice and Guidance Only:*
   — where no referral or direction is appropraite or possible — discussion of alternative plans and provide brief counselling.

4. *Information obtained by Information London:*
   — information centre on behalf of an enquirer has to get or provide information that should be readily available. Enquirer may express dissatisfaction with information obtained, or some other difficulty in obtaining information from an agency or service he has contacted.

5. *Other:*
   — where a person refuses service or hangs up.

6. *Referral or Direction Back:*
   — where appropriate action is a referral or direction back to an agency or other resource to which the enquirer is known or with which he has had recent contact.

7. *Referral (Information London made contact):*
   — where information centre makes contact with an agency or resource.

8. *Service Performed:*
   — where the information centre performs a service such as helping to fill out forms, providing interpreter service, etc.

APPENDIX 3B
Category of Inquiry and Age

	10–19		20–29		30–39		40–49		50–59		60–69		70+		Total	
Accommodation	13	8.1	26	6.0	13	4.0	8	4.0	6	5.1	4	4.9	0	0.0	70	5.3
Adjustment	1	0.6	5	1.1	3	0.9	5	2.5	1	0.9	0	0.0	0	0.0	15	1.1
Child Welfare	0	0.0	9	2.1	5	1.5	2	1.0	2	1.7	0	0.0	0	0.0	18	1.3
Employment & Vocational	18	11.3	24	5.5	13	4.0	12	6.0	6	5.1	1	1.3	0	0.0	74	5.5
Financial	5	3.1	42	9.7	15	4.6	19	9.6	13	11.1	9	11.1	3	13.6	106	7.9
Health	10	6.3	24	5.5	27	8.3	10	5.0	4	3.4	7	8.6	2	9.2	84	6.3
Home Services	2	1.3	5	1.1	8	2.5	4	2.0	4	3.4	6	7.4	0	0.0	29	2.2
Landlord/Tenant	6	3.7	35	8.0	27	8.3	14	7.0	7	6.0	7	8.6	1	4.5	97	7.2
Consumer	10	6.3	44	10.1	43	13.3	28	14.2	20	17.1	17	21.0	5	22.8	167	12.5
Education	9	5.6	14	3.2	14	4.3	4	2.0	1	0.9	0	0.0	0	0.0	42	3.1
Legal	9	5.6	24	5.5	20	6.2	9	4.5	7	6.0	0	0.0	1	4.5	70	5.3
Other	12	7.6	39	9.0	29	9.0	18	9.0	9	7.7	6	7.4	4	18.2	117	8.7
General	21	13.1	43	9.9	30	9.3	26	13.1	8	6.8	8	9.9	4	18.2	140	10.5
Dental Care	0	0.0	0	0.0	2	0.6	0	0.0	2	1.7	0	0.0	0	0.0	4	0.3
Gov't. Service Info.	4	2.5	10	2.3	12	3.8	4	2.0	3	2.6	1	1.3	0	0.0	34	2.5
Recreation & Vacation	39	24.4	79	18.3	58	17.9	33	16.6	24	20.5	12	14.8	1	4.5	246	18.4
Immigration	0	0.0	1	0.2	0	0.0	0	0.0	0	0.0	0	0.0	0	0.0	1	0.1
Pollution	1	0.6	11	2.5	5	1.5	3	1.5	0	0.0	3	3.7	1	4.5	24	1.8
Total	160	100.0	435	100.0	324	100.0	199	100.0	117	100.0	81	100.0	22	100.0	1,338	100.0

About the Author

Benjamin D. Singer is a member of the Sociology Department, The University of Western Ontario and has been the Lincoln Filene Visiting Professor at Dartmouth College. He received his B.A. from Wayne State University and the M.A. and Ph.D. from the University of Pennsylvania in 1965. Dr. Singer has been consultant to Children's Psychiatric Research Institute and to the Department of Communications of the Canadian Government. He is the author, senior author or editor of the books *Black Rioters, Radio in a Community Emergency, Communications in Canadian Society,* as well as having written articles on psychiatry, mass society and communications in various scholarly journals.

Index

"Access to Information: A Position Paper on Communications Channels and Social Change," 63
"Action Line," 15
Alinsky, Saul, 6
Allinson, Nina, xi
Almond, Gabriel A., and Sidney Verba, 3, 9
"America's Town Meeting of the Air," 9
Anomie, 57–62
Arendt, Hannah, 2

Bauer, Raymond A., 3
Bogart, Leo, 12–13
Boulding, Kenneth E., 1, 4, 91–92
British Citizens Advice Bureaux, 18
Buckley, William F., 14, 15

CFPL, 29, 45
CJOE, 29, 45
CKSL, 29, 45
"Call for Action," 17–18, 93–94
Call-in shows, radio, 15–18, 21, 22, 29, 45–56, 85, 87; and anomie, 60; topics of calls to, 97–99, 103–6
Canada Council, xi
Cleveland, James C., 3
Coding analyses, 95–106, 109–15
Constable, Rosalind, 14
Coughlin, Father, 10
Crittenden, John, 16, 17

Davis and Rarick, 13
Detroit Free Press, 15
Deutsch, Karl W., 88
Durkheim, 57

Feedback: analysis of, 21–32; research in, 9–20; uses of, 1–7
Forsythe, Sidney A., 11, 13
Foster and Friedrich, 13, 52, 62
Future Shock, 1, 14

Ginsberg, Allen, 14
Green, Lyndsay, xi
Grey, David L., and Trevor R. Brown, 10, 12, 13, 52
Guité, Michael, 3
Gwyn, Richard, xi

Hannigan, Andrew, xi
Hannigan, John A., 15, 41, 42–43, 59
Harper's, 14
Head, Wilson A., 18

Helling, R. A., 18
Hooper, Charles, 12
Houston Chronicle, 15

Information centers, 18–19, 29–30, 90–91; topics of calls to, 109–15
Information London, 30–32, 67–84
Ironside, Diana J., 18

Jackson, Elton, 37
Jaspers, Karl, 88
Johnson, Nicholas, 18
Johnston, Dale, xi

KABC, 16
Kahn, Alfred J., 6, 70
Kitto, H.D.F., 2
Kline, Alan, 12
Knight, Bud, xi

Leary, Timothy, 14
Lewis, Anthony, 11, 13
Letter writers, 34–37; topics of, 95–96
London Free Press, xi, 11, 22, 33, 41, 63, 85
London, Ontario, 19, 21–32; newspaper ombudsman in, 41–44; radio call-in show in, 45–56; and see London Free Press; "Sound Off"
Love, Kenny, 14

McEachern, Margaret, 16
Machlup, Fritz, 18
Mailer, Norman, 14
Meier, Richard L., 1, 88
Michigan Survey Research Center, 12
Mills, C. Wright, 2, 88
Montagu, Ashley, 14

Neighborhood Information Centers, 18
Neuman, Franz, 2
New York Post, 12, 14
New York Times, 10–11, 12, 14
Newspaper ombudsmen, 14–15, 41–44
Newspapers, letters to, 10–14, 33–40; and anomie, 58–59
Newsweek, 12, 16

Olson, David J., 10
"Open Line," 45, 60
Orillia Packet and Times, 12

Polls, 3–4

Product and Distribution of Knowledge in the United States, The, 18
Public Opinion Quarterly, 16
Puerto Rico, Study of, 4

Radio call-in shows, *see* Call-in shows, radio
Robinson, John P., and Philip R. Shaver, 57
Rosenau, 12
Rosenthal, Irving, 11–12

St. Catherines Standard, 12
Sanderson, Gordon, 41
Sayre, Jeanette, 9
Schiller, Herbert I., 3
Seacrest, Ted, xi
Silvers, Bob, 14
Singer, Benjamin D., 5, 14, 63
Singer, Benjamin D., and Cameron, 12, 63
Skornia, Harry, 91
Smith, Larry, 12
"Sound Off," 41–44, 60, 61–62, 85, 86, 87; and anomie, 59–60
"Speak Out," 16
Srole, Leo, 57
Srole scale, 58–62
Steven, Bill, 15
Stevens, Chandler, xi, 2, 4, 5

Stewart, Gail, and Cathy Stars, 18
Stratford Beacon Herald, 12
Sussman, Leila, 9, 10, 13, 14

Telegram, 12
Time, 14
Times (London), 11
Today's Health, 16
Toffler, Alvin, xi, 1, 6, 14
Topics: of inquiries to information center, 109–15; of letter writers, 95–96; of radio call-in shows, 97–99, 103–6
Toronto Globe and Mail, 10, 11, 33

Umpleby, Steward A., 4–5

Vacin, Gary L., 11, 13

WMCA, 93–94
WWDC, 18
Wagner, Robert, 93
"Watchem," 15
"Why Don't We Complain?", 14
Wiener, Norbert, 2
Wolfson, Marvin, 12
Wyant, and Herzog, 13